HER REFLECTION
OF HIS IMAGE

By

Carolyn Priest

ISBN: 0-89137-465-5

Dedication

Lovingly dedicated to my mother who continually
reflects God's image.

Acknowledgments

My deepest thanks to:
Marla Walters, Dorothy Wright, Louine Woodruff,
Marilyn Dowdy and Travis Thompson:
your suggestions and help were invaluable.

Judy King and Jane Sharp (cousins)
and Doris Romine (sister):
your stimulating ideas triggered many thoughts
for this book

My four daughters; Theresa, Cheryl, Matilda and Laurie:
your encouragement and love helped me to persevere.

Dean Priest Jr. (son):
without your patience in teaching computer skills my
book would still be on scratch paper.

Special thanks to Dean Priest Sr., my dear husband:
your confidence in my ability spurred me on
to completion.

TABLE OF CONTENTS

Bible Versions Used

INTRODUCTION

As a woman, my most noble goal is to function as I was intended to function in the eyes of God who created me: to mirror his view of me clearly and undistortedly to the world. To do this effectively, it becomes my responsibility to see myself as God sees me.

Michelangelo, famous artist and sculptor, when asked how he created such wonderful masterpieces is said to have replied, "God put them in the stone. All I did was let them out." Of course, it takes the eye of an artist to perceive the beauty in the stone and to "let it out." I, in my full potential, am in the eyes of my creator. He sees in me an abundant, radiant, fulfilled Christian. My hindrance in becoming may be one of perceptual vision. I can only reflect God's view of womanhood to the world to the extent that I perceive it.

The famous poet, **Robert Burns**, once said, "Oh, wad some Pow'r the Giftee gie us to see oursels as others see us."[1]

A more noble wish, it seems, would be to see myself as God sees me, for only as I see, can I be. Created in the image of God, it becomes my primary responsibility to know him, for it is in knowing him that I can reflect his image.

The urgency of knowing God was impressed

1

upon me in a youth gathering on New Year's Eve, 1959. We sat in a circle reciting our resolutions for the new year, all focusing on our anticipated accomplishments and growth; to pray more, to read more, to be aware of others, to attend worship services faithfully, to control tongue and temper. The youth director, my own beloved uncle, was asked, "Sir, what is your resolution?" He responded simply, "I want to know God more fully than I've ever known him." I pondered this thought a moment and noted that this compelling desire to know God bore witness in his image. It was easy to see God through him, for his life was dedicated to worshipping God and conveying his presence to others through the avenue of song.

The purpose of this study, then, is to help us to know God more perfectly and by knowing him to reflect his image in our lives, becoming all that he would have us to be. How is this to be accomplished? Paul tells us in 2 Corinthians 3:18, "But we all, with unveiled face, beholding as in a mirror the glory of the Lord, are being transformed into the same image from glory to glory, just as by the Spirit of the Lord."

As a mirror can only reflect my image when my face is turned in its direction, so I reflect God's image only when my eyes are fixed on him.

Too often our faces are veiled and our view of God is obscured by the many activities of the day. The force to *do* rather than to *be* has overtaken us. We are being told by the world that busier is better and that accomplishment is the essence of life.

Jesus, the epitomy of power to accomplish, spent many hours in the mountain alone with God, observing his handiwork: the lilies of the field and the birds of the air. He communed with God. Knowing God and being with God were his priorities.

Mary was extolled by Jesus because she gave priority to observing, listening and becoming while her sister, Martha, was kindly rebuked for her obsession with doing. I can relate to this trait of Martha's. While I want to spend time with my Creator, I find myself sandwiching him in between housework, the overseeing of rental property, visits with our sick and aged parents, time spent with my grandchildren, and trips taken with my husband. Where is the time to experience the mystery and wonder of God?

We are admonished, "Be still and know that I am God" (Psa. 46:10). Only when activity is laid aside will knowing God become our priority, for it is in stillness that we perceive most, and in silence that we hear best. So, let us lie beside the still waters and reflect on God, his nature, his essence, his very being to such an extent that we will be transformed into his likeness.

A Sunday school student once made this statement, "We hear a lot about God, the father, but what about God, the mother?" I thought on this at length. While God's qualities are neither masculine nor feminine, applying to man and woman alike, there are some traits that we, as women, do relate to in a unique way. In this study each chapter group will include an examination of one aspect of God's nature followed by a study of woman's efforts to imitate this quality in her life. Hopefully, this study will elevate our perception of womanhood and help us get beyond the mold of mundaneness by seeing something beautiful and noble in our daily routines.

Silence

In silence comes all loveliness
The dawn is ever still,
No noise accompanies the dew
That glistens on the hill.

The sunrise comes up quietly
The moon is never heard,
And love that animates the eyes
Surpasses any word.

And prayer is best in solitude,
It seems so very odd
That long before I did not know,
In silence I'd find God.[2]

1. Robert Burns, "To a Louse," *Norton Anthology of English Literature* (Norton, New York: M. H. Abrams, 1986) p. 236.
2. Andy T. Ritchie Jr., *Thou Shalt Worship The Lord Thy God* (Austin, Texas: Firm Foundation Pub. Co., 1969), pp. 36, 37. Used by permission.

CREATING

Chapter One

GOD, THE CREATOR

In our effort to behold God it is appropriate to start at the beginning. God, through his son, Jesus, created all things. "For by Him all things were created, that are in heaven and that are on earth, visible and invisible, whether thrones, or dominions, or principalities or powers. All things were created through Him, and for Him" (Col l:l6).

God, then, is not *a* creator, but *the* creator. He is the **Alpha** and **Omega**, the beginning and the end. This rules out all origins but God. He is the only creator. As we look closely at God, the creator, certain aspects of his creative nature unfold.

God is Visionary

Everything we are and have and know originated in the mind of God. Vision precedes product. Artists are aware of this. **Lee Watts**, outstanding current Arkansas artist, states that envisioning the finished product is the most difficult part of painting. After he clearly envisions the painting in its finished form, putting it on canvas is relatively easy.

Even while the earth was drab and dark God envisioned beauty and light. And what a product resulted! His artistic eye added the perfect touch of color, blends which artists throughout all ages have attempted to recapture: lightning interspersing a storm, a rainbow brightening a gray cloudy sky, birds of brilliant shades of red and blue feeding midst a white, snow-covered world, crimson clover blossoming in a deep green background, a lone desert flower springing up in a barren area.

God saw void, but he envisioned fullness. He envisioned a universe filled with sensations which appeal to each of our senses: rich and beautiful sounds such as the rippling waters, the ocean's roar, and the birds' chorus; sweet smells of honeysuckle and freshly cut hay; the softness of a baby's kiss, a warm hand-clasp; and the taste of cool water to a parched mouth.

The fullness which God envisioned also included mankind made in his image, equipped with his potential for love and joy. His vision, however, also allowed him to see the fall of man and his need for reinstatement and redemption. Therefore, his fullness included a plan for salvation, one of the greatest marvels of creation.

Knowing that you were not redeemed with corruptible things, like silver or gold, from your aimless conduct received by tradition from your fathers, but with the precious blood of Christ, as of a lamb without blemish and without spot. He indeed was foreordained before the foundation of the world, but was manifest in these last times for you. (I Pe. I:l8-20)

6

And all who dwell on the earth will worship him, whose names have not been written in the Book of Life of the Lamb slain from the foundation of the world. (Rev. 13:8)

God saw chaos, but envisioned order. This order included changing seasons, daily weather, differing climates, and a diversity of flowers, trees, and animals, each appropriate for its natural habitat, birds that fly under the direction of their own flight engineer, and bees that work by meticulous plan.

He also envisioned order for the home, giving it structure so that it would function as he intended it to. Man's nature called for a forefront position and God chose him to be head of the home, his makeup being such that he could accept the responsibilities and demands accompanying that job.

Woman, with an ability to cope with trivial crises, a special tenderness, and an eye for beauty, was placed inside the home unit to become its heart. She would not be placed here as punishment, nor to deprive her of the glory and honor of a forefront position, but to reward her with the love and praise of those dearest to her, husband and children who "rise up and call her blessed" (Prov. 31:28).

Children would be given to complete the home unit. They were God's way of affirming the ongoing process of life.

This family unit, or home, was envisioned to be the utopian setting for procreating life and happiness. God's vision was clear and his plan set before creation began.

Joy in Creation

God enjoyed creating. Each day of creation

ended with an exclamation of satisfaction, "It is good!" He liked what he made, and he said so. We can imagine the satisfaction that could be gained by such a magnificent creation. It contained the perfect balance of textures and temperatures, color and design. He, being endowed with the same senses that we know and enjoy, must have revelled in the sights, sounds, and smells of the universe.

We are made to wonder exactly what the purpose of creation was unless it was for pleasure. God, being all sufficient, had no needs to satisfy. Yet, we are told that all things were created *for* him. We could suppose, then, that he chose to express his creativity in a fulfilling and productive way simply for pleasure. "For thou hast created all things and for thy pleasure they are and were created" (Rev. 4:ll KJV).

God's joy was so great that he longed to share his pleasure in the newly created universe, and so he created man. We, as women, can understand this desire. Half the joy in giving birth to a baby is found in sharing this special moment with those we love, those whom we know will also love and appreciate this tiny gift of life. My husband and I waited at the hospital for the birth of our first grandchild. When our daughter was finally wheeled into the hall with a beaming husband at her side and a baby girl nestled on her breast the four of us shed tears of joy together. We were bonded in love because of our mutual pleasure in this new creation.

Mark Twain once said, "To get the full value of joy you must have somebody to divide it with."[1] We can picture God sharing his pleasure in the universe with Adam and Eve as they walked in the garden in the cool of the day, feeling a gentle breeze blowing, smelling the aroma of fruit blossoms, and perhaps viewing a beautiful sunset.

God added the extra flourish to life that makes each of us able to exclaim, "It is good!" His world was not only functional, but aesthetically beautiful and rich. He added those little extras that make life good, that serve no other purpose than pleasure. For example, there is joy of taste. Plants get nourishment without taste buds and supposedly, so could we. Life, however, is much happier because of the joy we experience in taste. The satisfaction gained from a good meal on an otherwise bland and uneventful day can add zest to life.

God could have chosen countless ways to perpetuate life, but he chose the intimacy of sex to give increased pleasure. This was one of the little *extras* given to ensure our joy in his creation.

Throughout time God has continued to enjoy man's pleasure in his creation. From David's psalms extolling the creation and the Creator to present day composers of Christian music and literature, we see an ongoing, mutual pleasure in God's creation uniting man and God in a common mindset.

Creator of Creativity

Having experienced, himself, the joy of creating, he endowed each of us with seeds of creativity also. He created us to be creative! Gifts of imagination, curiosity, and invention were planted in us in order that we might experience the same satisfaction in creativity that he experienced. Each of us has a contribution to make to the world. **Calvin Miller**, current artist and author, stated, "Our calling to paint or sing or play or dance is not the Great Commission, but it is a worthy commission that cries "Go! Make the world more beautiful!" [2]

Perhaps it is in the creation of ideas that mankind

becomes most like his creator. Many great men and women have recognized their ideas as stemming from God, not self. **Fanny Crosby**, composer of many well-known hymns, believed that many of the song lyrics were given to her by God. She felt incapable of creating these alone. **Tolkein**, creator of children's myths, called his myths "inventions of truth," and he felt that they "reflect a splintered fragment of eternal truth that is with God." He believed that through myth making he became a subcreator. Writing was for him a form of worship. He stated, "We make in our measure and derivative mode because we are made: and not only made, but made in the image and likeness of our Maker."[3]

The most mystical of the creative potentials God gave to woman was that of giving birth. Through the birth process she becomes a partaker with God in creation. Her body is " fearfully and wonderfully made,"[4] the womb perfectly acclimated for nurturing and sustaining life. What a privilege it is to be a part of his ongoing creation!

Behold, children are a heritage from the Lord, the fruit of the womb is His reward. Like arrows in the hands of a warrior so are the children of one's youth. Happy is the man who has his quiver full of them. (Psa.127:3-4)

After creating the home unit to serve as a perpetual creation center God pronounced his creation *very good!* It climaxed his creation.

God's Constant Awareness

Another trait of creativity which we can observe in God is his awareness. He is continually aware of his creation. He knows the names of the stars and the

10

number of hairs in our heads. He notes each sparrow that falls to the ground. Citing the attentiveness given to the lilies of the field and the birds of the air he promises to watch even more carefully over his children.

Now, if God so clothes the grass of the field, which today is, and tomorrow is thrown into the oven, will He not much more clothe you, O you of little faith? (Matt. 6:30)

God's constant attention and solicitous care are noted by David.

He will not allow your foot to be moved: He who keeps you will not slumber. Behold, he who keeps Israel shall neither slumber nor sleep. The Lord is your keeper: the Lord is your shade at your right hand. The sun shall not strike you by day, nor the moon by night. The Lord shall preserve you from all evil: He shall preserve your soul. The Lord shall preserve your going out and your coming in from this time forth, and even forevermore. (Psa. l21:3-8)

His eyes and ears are ever tuned to our needs. "The eyes of the Lord are on the righteous and his ears are open to their cry" (Psa. 34:15).

God is even aware of the center of our emotions and our moral sensitivity. "For you formed my inward parts; you have covered me in my mother's womb" (Psa. l39:13).

"O Lord, you have searched me and known me. You know my sitting down and my rising up; You understand my thoughts afar off" (Psa. l39:1-2).

God's constant awareness of my presence, my needs, and my every action affords great security.

Knowing that our creator is never off duty, that he never loses interest, never wearies, and never overlooks, should free us from an obsession with our own well-being. We should be more light-hearted than the birds of the air because we enjoy an even greater share of God's attention than they.

We cannot escape God's awareness even if we try. The whole universe offers no hiding place from God. This should serve as a great comfort to us.

Where can I go from Your spirit? Or where can I flee from Your presence? If I ascend into heaven, You are there; If I make my bed in hell, behold, You are there. If I take the wings of the morning, and dwell in the uttermost parts of the sea; Even there Your hand shall lead me, and Your right hand shall hold me.
(Psa. 139:7-10)

Creativity Implies Uniqueness

Uniqueness is an aspect of God's creativity that intrigues us. He did not go into mass production, but formed each person with an individual image, (though made in the image of God), peculiar gifts, potential for learning and achieving, and a personal level of accomplishment. To some he gave a musical talent, to others an orator's tongue. Some were blessed with athletic prowess, others with a writer's fluency or an artistic eye.

This uniqueness of creation is a marvel. A small two year old granddaughter comes to me with pencil and paper saying, "Grandmother, draw people, draw people." I, being no artist, draw the same little stick body, round head, eyes, nose and mouth which invariably fall in the same location each time, causing all of my people to look just alike. Then I put long curly hair to identify the girls and short crew cuts to identify the boys. I often stop to wonder at a God who has formed billions of people throughout the ages, no two having the same fingerprints, much less the same mind. A God, concerned enough to give to each person individual physical characteristics, intellectual potential, and personality certainly has different expectations and plans for his or her accomplishment. Each has an individual role to play in life.

God's interaction with man is as colorful and unique as is his design. In Bible times he used original, one-of-a-kind methods of communication. He revealed himself to Moses in a burning bush. Saul's call came with a blinding light and a voice from Heaven (Acts 9:3), and Jacob's from an angel-filled ladder (Gen. 28:12, 13). Samuel heard a strange voice in the night (1 Sam. 3:4), and Mary was visited by an angel (Luke 1:28). Each was an out-of-the-ordinary experience.

God has also used unique and surprising evidences to speak his power and presence. A contest held on Mt. Carmel proved that God could produce rock-eating fire while Baal could not produce (1 Kings 18:21-29). Even when coming to earth to reveal himself to us as man he didn't come as the expected king robed in purple, but rather as a babe wrapped in swaddling clothes, born to common folk. When Jesus hung on the cross the people sought evidence as to his origin by asking him to come down from the cross, but God used his own ingenious evidence instead, ripping the veil of the temple and letting the dead walk the city streets of Jerusalem (Matt. 27:52-53).

Creative methods of discipline were devised by

God. He had no stale, set of rules, but chose methods appropriate for the behavior. Jonah's attempt to evade God was thwarted by a big fish. Three dark, cold, and wet days reversed his behavior (Jon. 1:17). The Israelites were made to taste the bitterness of their sin by drinking the ground-up calf they had worshipped (Ex. 32:20), and David lost the baby which was the fruit of his desire (2 Sam. 12:18). Cain's mark, Herod's worms, and Miriam's leprosy were other examples of God's unique discipline.

God's Ongoing Creation

Creativity is not only a thing of the past, but a part of God's nature. Whenever we see a bulb unfold into a flower, or an egg crack open to expel a baby chicken, when we hear a newborn baby's cry, or a bird's new song, we are reminded that reproduction continues.

It is hard for us to conceive of a creation superior to this universe. Yet, it exists in promise. John's brief glimpse into God's glorious creation of Heaven assures us of the perpetuality of creation.

But be glad and rejoice forever in that which I create, for behold I create Jerusalem a rejoicing and her people a joy. (Isa. 65:18)RSV

And he carried me away in the Spirit to a great and high mountain and showed me that great city, the holy Jerusalem, descending out of heaven from God. (Rev. 21:10)

Conclusion

No matter how colorful and exciting God's

creation of the universe, how perfect his design of the home, or of the eternal home, it would hold no significance at all, as far as I am concerned, except that he also created *me.* For this I am very grateful. He entrusted my birth, care, and teaching to godly, middle-class parents who, though poor in this world's goods, were rich in love for God, their fellowman, each other and me. What a wonderful endowment this was!

It becomes my responsibility, then, as well as yours, to discover my potential for accomplishment, the specific niche formed for me in life, and to live according to the expectations of my creator.

I. Glenn VanEkeren, *The Speaker's Sourcebook* (Englewood Cliffs, New Jersey: Prentice Hall, 1988). Used by permission.
2. Calvin Miller, "Created to Create", *Decision,* Oct., 1988, Billy Graham Evangelistic Assoc., p. 38. Used by permission. All rights reserved.
3. Janice S. Okulski, "J. R. R. Tolkien," *Eternity* , Sept., 1984, Evangelical Ministries, Inc., Phil., Pa., p.35. Reprinted by permission.
4. Psalm 139:14

THOUGHTS FOR DISCUSSION

1. Is society, as a whole, functioning as God envisioned it? If not, what forces are responsible for its malfunctioning?
2. What can be done to make God's awareness of us and his presence with us more real?
3. Thought for consideration: If God's universe, which was created in seven days and will exist for only a short time, is so pleasant and beautiful, how much more appealing Heaven, in its state of perfection, must be!
4. Discuss some of the ways in which Heaven is superior to this universe as noted in:
   Isa. 65:17-24
   Rev. 22:3-5
   Rev. 21:4
   Rev. 21:22-25
5. Given my unique background and potentials, what does God expect of me that he may not expect of anyone else in the world?

Prayer Thought: "Thank you, Lord, for your marvelous creation, a creation which included me. Help me to be what you created me to be."

Chapter Two

CREATED, YET CREATIVE

To create means to bring into being, to originate or to design. In the true sense of the word I can create nothing, for I, and all that I accomplish, originated in God. God is the only creator.

Though I cannot create like God, I am endowed with certain creative potentials, one being that of sharing with God in the process of giving life. Bringing into the world an immortal soul, aware that I am a primary determining agent as to where this soul will spend eternity, is an awesome task! It is one that calls for all my creative abilities.

Creativity is in no way confined to parenting. Our creative potentials can be utilized in every area of Christian service. There are many "Annas" serving God continually through means other than the home. One does not have to be a wife or mother in order to be creative, or pleasing to God. However, the aspect chosen for emphasis in this chapter is creative parenting. The characteristics of creativity discussed here hopefully can be employed in other aspects of our lives as well.

Society today does not hold motherhood in the

same esteem that it once did. Careers of many kinds take precedence over child-rearing. Preschools, day-care centers and babysitting agencies are thriving while mother-care is on the decline. Why is the role of full-time mother no longer pursued by the majority of women? There are many women who long to devote full time to their children but are unable to do so because of life's circumstances. They must devise creative ways to utilize every bit of energy and time to meet the challenges before them, and they can do it with God's help. There are others, however, who entrust the teaching and training of their children to strangers simply because they fail to see the significance of their jobs at home.

Be Visionary!

As God was visionary in his creativity so we must be in ours seeing the role of motherhood as God designed it to be. He gave us the most stimulating and challenging job in the world. Communicating God to my own children may be my best means of carrying out the great commission, my chief outreach to future generations. Through Timothy the faith of Eunice and Lois touched the entire world. An old English proverb says, "Any fool can count the seeds in an apple. Only God can count the number of apples in a seed." When my children were quite young I carefully observed an older lady whom I considered to be an ideal parent model [a very successful mother of four.] "What is your secret in parenting? " I asked. "No special secret," she replied. "But, we do try to rear our children in such a way that our grandchildren will be saved." That's vision! Today's behavior becomes one small stepping stone toward the finished product, which lies in the future generation.

God chose Mary to be the mother of his son. Perhaps it was her vision which best qualified her for this job,. She was aware of the long range significance of his birth. Though single and surprised, she accredited this baby, this tiny gift of life, to be a blessing from God for all generations to come. Her song of praise gives insight into her attitude.

My soul magnifies the Lord and my spirit has rejoiced in God my Savior,. For He has regarded the low estate of His maid servant; For behold, henceforth all generations will call me blessed. For He who is mighty has done great things for me and holy is His name. (Lk. I:46-49)

Abraham was chosen by God to be the father of the Jewish nation. One of the criteria for selection lay in his ability to command his children and his children's children after him. He was not short sighted (Gen. 18:19).

Jochebed was visionary. She was cited in the book of Hebrews because of her willingness to forego her own safety and life, if necessary, to nurture a son whom she believed to be no ordinary child, but a special gift from God.

By faith Moses, when he was born, was hidden three months by his parents, because they saw he was a beautiful child, and they were not afraid of the king's command. (Heb. 11:23)

Jochebed was successful in transmitting her vision to her son.

...esteeming the reproach of Christ greater riches than the treasures in Egypt, for he *looked to the reward.* By faith he forsook Egypt, not fearing the wrath of the king; for he endured as *seeing Him who is invisible.* (Heb. ll:26-27)

It takes vision to persevere in our jobs. Sometimes we are plagued with myopia. Today's behavior can override tomorrow's dream. We see only the crayon marks on the wallpaper, the temper tantrum in the store, the getting out of bed for one last forbidden drink, or the refusal to say "thank you." Discouragement can overtake us.

Our Father has distant vision. He sees us veer. He sees us fail. Yet, he never gives up. We are his chosen vessels, set apart, redeemed. We simply have our bad days and he picks us up and steers us on. We, as parents, must do the same. We must keep our eye on the finished product and not on the small, daily picture. Seeing our children for what God created them to be will help obliterate the ugly picture of imperfect development during the interim stages.

Value Uniqueness

Creative parenting certainly implies valuing the individuality and originality in each child. God gave us original material to work with, each child being God's patented formula, a one of a kind, unique package. Each has peculiar talents, intellect, personality, appearance and environment. What works for one child won't necessarily work for another. What works for one mother won't necessarily work for another. We must search for the individuality in each of our children so that we can help them to be what God created them to be.

A family moved to a new community. The mother was eager to know how her son was performing in the new school system. She went in for a conference and was told by the teacher, "He's just an average child from an average country school. Nothing special." What a sad misconception! This teacher was unable to see the individuality, the beauty, the potential in one of God's creations. She didn't recognize his worth. I'm glad God doesn't compare us to, nor measure us by, any other being. I'm glad he can see the little bit of "special" in each of us. He doesn't count any one of his children "just average."

Herman Mellville said, "It is better to fail in originality than to succeed in imitation."[1] Each child needs experiences appropriate for developing his own individual interests. Organized group projects may offer little opportunity for originality. We are often inclined to fill our lives and the lives of our children so full of planned activities which, though good, are not necessarily the best use of time. Boy Scouts, Girl Scouts, swimming lessons, piano lessons, Parent Teacher meetings, and organized sports are juggled around meal time and school time until, as Pollyanna observed, there is scarcely time to "just live." Where is the time for daydreaming? For contemplation? Where is the time to *become?* Is it more important for our children to *do* or to *be?* Cluttering and overcrowding the environment may produce human *doers* rather than human *beings.* We must leave time for imagining, for visualizing, and for considering.

When individuals at various ages were tested for creativity, the results of the study were as follows:[2]

Age	How Many Are Creative
5	90%
17	10%
30	2%
35	2%
40	2%

These statistics indicate that between the ages of five and seventeen there is an extreme drop in the creative level in both male and female students. During that young, vulnerable growing period a "we are not creative" attitude takes over, and we begin to deny that particular part of our God-given equipment. What is happening during those years to squelch creativity? Why does conformity become the norm? It is important to help select experiences which deserve to be part of our children's lives.

School experiences which stagnate creativity are depicted in the song, "Flowers Are Red."

The little boy went first day of school
He got colors and he started to draw
He put colors all over the paper
For colors was what he saw
And the teacher said, "What 'cha doing young man?"
"I'm paintin' flowers," he said.
She said,"It's not the time for art young man
And anyway, flowers are green and red.
There's a time for everything young man
And a way it must be done
You've got to show concern for everyone else,
For you're not the only one."
She said,
"Flowers are red young man, and green leaves

are green,
There's no need to see flowers any other way
Than the way they always have been seen."

It becomes my responsibility to stimulate, not stagnate my children's ideas, and to provide experiences that will encourage them to pursue their own dreams. I want to value their creativity enough to see immediate productivity pushed aside for dreaming and envisioning. I want to appreciate all that is praiseworthy in them, to accept them as they are, and to help them accept themselves. In other words, I want to value their originality more than their conformity.

Make God-awareness a Priority

Making our children aware of God is a most important element in creative child rearing. If I am aware of God in all of my surroundings I can communicate him to my children from an early age. Our homes are too silent to God. We need to verbalize our awareness of him, calling attention to the world around us, and praising God for its existence. As they observe the rain, the sunshine, sleet and snow they can be made aware of God, the Creator.

My daddy was a farmer. We lived close to the soil and to nature. God became very real in our home, operating in every phase of our lives. Daddy accredited the changing seasons, the rain and drought, the abundant harvests and the killing frosts to God. I seldom saw a summer rain without seeing him standing in its midst looking up to the sky to watch the clouds and exclaiming over the goodness of God in sending rain. He pointed out the meticulous design of creation on many occasions: the birds flying south in perfect formation, the squirrels burying their nuts in autumn

23

(God's way of planting the forests), the bees working with plan and design. My daddy's faith was evident to me from the time I was a young child.

There is a story told of a young man who longed to see God. He had heard for many years of a wise old man who lived in the mountains nearby. After searching elsewhere for God in vain, the young man finally went to talk with the old man. "Old man, tell me, how can I see God?" The old man stopped, and looked at him deeply. He immersed himself in thought. The young man waited for what seemed like an eternity. Finally: "Young man, I don't think that I can be of help to you, for you see I have a problem that is quite different. I can't help but see Him." This man saw God in the whole universe. We want our children to do the same. We cannot *assume* their faith. We must make every effort to *assure* it.

God-awareness is best achieved in a home climate where children are encouraged to ponder God. The mother plays a dominant role in setting the atmosphere and mood. A home needs the proper balance of quietness, orderliness and free time to be conducive to thought. A rigid, highly structured, overly organized home can stifle God-awareness, while a disheveled, chaotic one can overwhelm it. I have longed for the wisdom of Solomon to achieve the proper balance.

God-awareness not only comes through a conducive home environment, but through direct teaching.

> And these words which I command you today shall be in your hearts; you shall teach them diligently to your children and shall talk of them when you sit in your house, when you walk by the way, when

you lie down, and when you rise up. You shall bind them as a sign and they shall be as frontlets between your eyes. You shall write them on the doorposts of your house and on your gates. (Deut. 6:6-9)

These commandments show that awareness of God must be a priority in our homes. It is challenging to find creative ways of communicating God to our children. Games are a good way to teach facts. Our entire family enjoyed games while traveling such as creating modern day parables, completing Bible verses, and playing our favorite game, *I Have a Character.* The one who is *IT* says, "I have a character." Then he describes the character, giving one clue at a time until someone guesses correctly. The one who guesses then becomes *IT.* We also used letters of the alphabet to play I'm Thinking of an A, (or R, or S etc.). The letter could stand for Bible names, books, or places. It was so much fun, as a child, to play this with my grandmother. My sister and I would search for unfamiliar Bible names to surprise her, so that P was not for the usual Peter or Paul but, rather for Peleg or Put.

Story-telling is an age old art which can make Bible characters come to life if the story is told enthusiastically. In the absence of man-made pictures the children form their own imagery, becoming active participants in the story.

We have a brief time to convey God's presence to our children and we need to select those routine moments of walking, sitting, and standing. It is more important to lay a strong foundation in faith than in the basic skills of education. Yet, we are sometimes more impressed with the necessity of learning the alphabet than the basic Bible facts.

25

Model Creativity

We, as mothers, must not only teach creatively, but we must model creativity in the home. Our children look to us for example as we look to God. Being able to accept and to generate new ideas is one aspect of creative thinking which we want to implement , but we may not find it easy to do. When our five children were at home it was easier to make the decisions myself than to listen to new and varying thoughts on how the household should be run. At one of our family conferences there was a general consensus that an earlier breakfast would help eliminate the getting off to school rush. Not being an early riser this was an unwelcome suggestion. Since, however, it had been brought up before the whole family and agreed upon, I had to rise to the occasion. Family conferences give each family member an opportunity to voice opinion and to give creative input into home management.

Modeling creativity involves showing a healthy attitude toward failure. We need to remind ourselves and our children that we are responsible for effort, not success. God may or may not bless our efforts with success. That is his part. Failure is sometimes acceptable, even commendable. **Thomas Edison** was once reminded that he failed 25,000 times while experimenting with the storage battery. "No, I didn't fail," the inventor replied. "I succeeded in finding 24,999 ways it does not work."[3] This healthy attitude toward failure gave him the incentive to persevere.

Another attempt to model creativity involves withholding judgment. In coping with the stresses of rearing four teenage girls I often found myself hasty in making decisions, and inclined to give quick, negative replies. **Dr. T. A. Formby**, our family physician and friend, offered a suggestion which was quite helpful. "Never give teenagers an immediate answer. Tell them you will need time to think on it. Then when you have had time to consider they will be willing to abide by your decision because they will know it was important to you." A hasty reply often meets with a harsh rebuttal. Impulsiveness shows little creativity.

It is also important to allow our children freedom to solve their own problems when possible. Direct answers and ready-made solutions merely stagnate their creativity, while providing a nurturing environment for their ideas and solutions stimulates thinking. Questions may be a good way to stimulate thought. "What is the purpose of your life?" or, "What did God create you to be?" may trigger a stimulating conversation or at least provide an idea to ponder.

It is not easy to let our children fight their own battles nor solve their own problems. **Catherine Marshall** says, "It is out of the pit of life that creativity is born, not in high places." [4] The pit is an unpleasant place to be. It is not pleasant to see my child there. But, if he comes out as a Joseph, aware that his life is being lived before God, then it has been the best breeding ground for creativity.

As a mentor I must also cultivate the seeds of creativity that are planted in me so that I will produce what God thinks worthy of being produced by me. Perhaps I can create stories, as Jesus did, which will pose problems to be faced, disappointments to be overcome, or dilemmas to be unraveled. If my gift is the ability to give wise counsel I must use it to uplift. The gift of counsel is no small gift, for God said, "Where there is no counsel, the people fall; but in the multitude of counselors there is safety" (Prov. 11:14). If I am gifted in music, I could use this gift to compose worshipful and inspiring songs as David did. I have a sister who has the ability to create gourmet meals and the generosity to share them with many people. She also has the ability to grow and arrange roses which are used to bless the sick, the grieved, the church assembly and many social events. Whether my creative ability is great or small I want to use it to bring glory to the Creator, not the created.

Conclusion

God gave us the most significant job in the world and left few instructions to accompany it because he knew that in an atmosphere of freedom we would function at our best. He told us to love, teach, and discipline - but he left the how up to us. He equipped us with the mental ability, however, to imagine, to generate ideas, to reason, and to inspire. In other words we were created to be creative! Let's unleash the imagination so that God's ultimate purposes for our lives and the lives of our children will be accomplished.

I. Glen Van Ekeren, *The Speaker's Sourcebook* (Englewood Cliffs, New Jersy: Prentice Hall, 1988). Used by permission.
2   Ibid., p 106.
3. Ibid., p. 157.
4. Catherine Marshall, *Beyond Ourselves* (Tarrytown, New York: Baker Book House Gleheida Pub. Group, 1961), p. 158. Used by permission.

THOUGHTS FOR DISCUSSION

1. Discuss the profession of motherhood: the versatility of talents and the expertise required in many areas. For example, a mother may well use training as a nutrition expert, nurse, piano teacher, educator, Bible teacher, nature specialist, seamstress and chef. List and discuss other talents useful in parenting.
2. What are some activities that could encourage creativity in your children at different stages?
   A. Preschool
   B. Gradeschool
   C. Teenage years
3. How can summer vacation be utilized for instilling creativity in children?
4. What was the most creative period in your life, and what were the circumstances surrounding it?
5. Discuss Psalm 139:13, "For you created my innermost being." Does this relate to our ability to create stories, music, art, and poetry?

Prayer Thought: " Make me aware of my creative potentials and help me to use them to bring glory to you."

NURTURING

Chapter Three

GOD, OUR EL SHADDAI

El is the standard name for God in the Old Testament, meaning "might" or "power." Shaddai means "breasted." It comes from the Hebrew word "Shad," that is, "the breast," or more exactly, a "woman's breast." **Kay Arthur**, in her book, **Lord, I Want To Know You**, found the term El Shaddai to mean literally, "All-Sufficient One".[1]

This term was first used when God revealed himself to Abraham in Genesis 17:1-3 as his El Shaddai. This revelation accompanied a promise to confirm his covenant, to increase his numbers, and to give him the promised land. As surely as God poured forth blessings for Abraham, becoming his El Shaddai, he nourishes us today. He satisfies our physical, emotional, and spiritual hunger.

Have you ever wondered why God created us with so many needs? Perhaps he knew that only in facing needs and in striving to meet those needs we would become aware of our insufficiency and fix our eyes on him.

Physical Nourisher

As a baby forms a strong attachment to his

30

mother by looking to her for physical nourishment so we are drawn closer to God by looking to him for daily care.

We may tend to think that physical nourishment is too finite to attract God's attention. We know this is untrue, however, when we consider his involvement in the physical needs of his children throughout time. He planted a garden for Adam and Eve and clothed them with skins (Gen. 2:8, 3:21). He rained down manna from heaven for the Israelites (Ex. 16:14, 15), and brought water from a rock (Ex. 17:6). He sent food to Elijah by the ravens (1 Kings 17:6), and replenished the widow's cruse of oil (1 Kings 17:4). He provided a fish for Jonah (Jon. 1:17), a cave for Elijah (1Kings 19:9), and a plan for an ark for Noah (Gen. 6:14).

Jesus involved himself in the physical aspect of ministry. He opened the eyes of the blind, healed the sick, raised the dead, and fed the multitude. His attention to the physical needs of others spoke care, concern, and love. There are several terms for Jesus which show his concern for physical needs.

The Bread of Life (John 6:48).

The Great Physician (John 5:8-9).

The Water of Life (John 7:37).

The True Vine (John 15:1).

The Good Shepherd (John 10:11).

Jesus showed awareness of God's being the source of our physical blessings by constantly thanking him for food and teaching us to pray for our daily bread (Matt. 6:11).

In today's world of supermarkets filled with canned goods, frozen goods and fresh produce shipped in from all parts of the world, we are farther removed from God, the direct provider. In days of self-contained farms where we grew what we ate and ate almost only what we grew, it was easier to see God's hand serving our table. Our meals reflected the weather which reflected God. A late freeze meant no peaches, pears, or apples. A severe cold spell was good "hog-killing" weather which provided a bounty of sausage, pork chops and bacon. The first frost in the fall brought an end to fresh garden vegetables and began the eating of canned and frozen foods which had been preserved for winter. Drought always brought scarcity of food and rain brought bounty.

Maltbie Babcock's verse states so well her awareness of the invisible God who is responsible for all of our daily provisions.

Back of the loaf is the snowy flour,
And back of the flour the mill,
And back of the mill is the wheat and the shower,

And the sun and the Father's will.[2]

In my childhood home it was inexcusable to complain about food. Since food was accredited to God it was to be accepted as a good gift. We were reminded of God's wrath toward the Israelites who longed for the fleshpots of Egypt when it was God's will they should eat manna instead (Ex.16:3, 4). It still seems ironic for a person to thank God for food in one breath and down-grade its quality in the next. God is an ample provider.

The awareness of God as the source of our physical nourishment releases us from the materialistic quest. It frees us from an obsession with our own provision, and allows us to seek first the kingdom of God and his righteousness with assurance that our physical needs will be met.

Therefore I say to you, do not worry about

your life, what you will eat, or what you will drink; nor about your body, what you will put on. Is not life more than food, and the body more than clothing? Look at the birds of the air; for they neither sow nor reap nor gather into barns; yet your Heavenly Father feeds them. Are you not of more value than they? So why do you worry about clothing? Consider the lilies of the field, how they grow: they neither toil nor spin. And yet I say to you that even Solomon in all his glory was not arrayed like one of these. Now if God so clothes the grass of the field, which today is and tomorrow is thrown into the oven, will He not much more clothe you, O you of little faith.Therefore do not worry saying, What shall we eat? or What shall we drink? or What shall we wear? For after all these things the Gentiles seek. For your heavenly Father knows that you need all these things. But seek first the kingdom of God and His righteousness, and all these things shall be added to you. (Matt. 6:25-26, 28-33.)

Emotional Nourisher

God nourishes us emotionally as well as physically. As a mother gives milk from her own body to satisfy her baby's physical hunger she also bonds with the child in love, satisfying the emotional hunger as well. God's love for us is our greatest source of emotional nourishment. He loves us unconditionally. He doesn't love us when, or because, or if, but he loves us in spite of, even though, and however. In our worship we proclaim our love to him. This is understandable. "God is love" (1 John 4:8). He is loving and lovable. The unfathomable thought is that God loves us, the unlovely, the unlovable.

It has been said that **Karl Barth**, well-known theologian, was asked to relate his most profound thought. After deliberation he replied, "Jesus loves me, this I know, for the Bible tells me so." What security there is in that thought!

As a child I heard an often used phrase at funeral services which stuck with me though it had little meaning to me then. The preacher would end his eulogy by saying, "Let's throw a cloak of charity over his faults and remember only his good." That phrase is quite meaningful today. In a sense that is God's response to us: He throws a cloak of charity over our faults and loves us in spite of them.

God's plan for our emotional nourishment included placing us inside a loving care group or family. It is here we should be loved most by those who know us best. It is here we should be accepted and valued. This environment affords the greatest amount of security.

In the children's book, **Miss Minerva and William Greenhill,** Billy, a recently orphaned five year old, was sent from a plantation where he had been cared for by a warm and loving Aunt Cindy, to live with his Aunt Minerva. Sleeping alone for the first time, in a dark room, he began to cry. "William," Aunt Minerva reminded him, "If you feel afraid just pray and God will hear you and take care of you." "I don't want no God," he replied firmly. "I want somebody with sho' nuff skin and bones."[3] In a sense the family is God's "sho nuff skin and bones." It is his love extended to us vicariously, an affirmation of his concern for our emotional well being.

The church family was also designed by God as a reinforcement of the family's love, to bear burdens, lift loads, and love without limit.   Its purpose was to provide the fellowship so needful for our emotional needs.

When the institutions of the home and church break down and fail to function as they were so designed, God's children starve emotionally. They are deprived of the love and concern which is necessary for stability. God is an ample provider! We, as humans, often fail to carry out his plan.

Discipline is another influence on our emotional stability, and God doesn't fail us in this area either.

My son, do not despise the chastening of the Lord, nor detest His correction; For whom the Lord loves He corrects, Just as a father the son in whom he delights. (Prov. 3:11-12)

Behold, happy is the man whom the Lord corrects. (Job 5:17)

My son, do not despise the chastening of the Lord, nor be discouraged when you are rebuked by Him: For whom the Lord loves He chastens, and scourges every son whom He receives. (Heb. 12:5-6)

As many as I love, I rebuke and chasten. (Rev. 3:19)

Every child feels insecure and unloved if he has

no one who cares enough to discipline him. When we consider hardships to be a form of discipline from a loving father we can accept them with appreciation, not resignation. They help to refine and perfect us. Sometimes God disciplines us directly and sometimes he prods us in the direction of self-discipline. We know that God does not tempt us with evil nor allow us to be tempted beyond our ability to resist, but he does allow us to pursue our sinful passions when we are intent on doing so. Does it seem strange that God did not let the rooster crow before Peter denied Christ rather than afterward? (Matt. 26:74) We may ask why Nathan wasn't sent to warn David before he took Bathsheba rather than after the fact. (2 Sam. 12:1)

There are times when our will is bent on doing wrong, and God lets us learn our own hard lessons. We sometimes have to go to the bottom before we begin to look upward. We don't see the same self-assured, pride-filled Peter after his sin that we saw before. We see, rather, a contrite, humbled man aware of his own ability to fall.

David could not have written the 51st Psalm, a prayer many of us have uttered in our grief over sin, unless he had been allowed to pursue his own way which led to the depths of sin.

Discipline is so important to each of us that God provided for it in his church. There is security in knowing fellow Christians care enough to discipline us when we stray. Each of us becomes an active participant in the emotional nourishment of the church in this way.

Spiritual Nourisher

While physical and emotional nourishment are important to God our spiritual welfare is of utmost importance to him. He made every provision possible for our salvation. Even before creation he devised a plan for our redemption. He would come and dwell among us in the person of his son. Emmanuel, "God with us", would live in our midst, involve himself in the lives of people, becoming himself a man. (Matt. 1:2-3, Isa. 7:14)

Max Lucado describes this event so beautifully in **God Came Near.**

> It all happened in a moment, a most remarkable moment...But in reality, that particular moment was like none other, for through that segment of time a spectacular thing occurred. God became a man. While the creatures of earth walked unaware, Divinity arrived. Heaven opened herself and placed her most precious one in a human womb.
> The omnipotent, in one instant, made himself breakable. He who had been spirit became pierceable. He who was larger than the universe became an embryo. And he who sustains the world with a word chose to be dependent upon the nourishment of a young girl. God as a fetus. Holiness sleeping in a womb. The creator of life being created.[4]

Jesus' ministry on earth was a spiritual one as well as a physical one. He became:
The Author and Perfector of our faith (Heb. 12:2).
The True Vine (John 15:1).
The Sacrificial Lamb (1Cor. 5:7).
The Good Shepherd (John 14:6).

The Way, the Truth, and the Life (John 14:6).

Are we of the 20th century deprived spiritually because we didn't live in the first century and become "eyewitnesses of His majesty?"⁵ No. If anything we are given a more complete view of him through the written accounts of various eyewitnesses. Through these accounts we can follow him into the Jordan River (Matt. 3:13), walk with him beside the Sea of Galilee (Matt. 15:29-30), sit at his feet in Bethany (Luke 10:39), sup with him in an upper room (Luke 22:12, 14), pray with him in the Garden (Luke 22:39-40), look into the empty tomb, and watch his ascension (John 24:50-51).

Not only do we have an account of his life, but a reminder of his physical presence as we eat the bread representing his life and drink the juice representing his blood. God knew that we would need a physical contact with him and so he instigated this feast called the Lord's Supper (Matt. 26:26-29).

One provision for our spiritual nourishment is God's willingness to adjust temptations to comply with our individual ability to resist. He does not promise to remove them, but he does promise to provide a way of escape, a deliverance. Knowing that the temptations we face have passed through God's hands and have been deemed suitable for us should give us confidence to triumph over evil.

> No temptation has overtaken you except such as is common to man; but God is faithful, who will not allow you to be tempted beyond what you are able, but with the temptation will also make the way of excape, that you may be able to bear it. (1 Cor. 10:13)

I am also firmly convinced that God gives us

some rich personal experiences, scattered throughout life, which are faith builders. These are the highlights which help sustain us in low ebbs of life. I'm sure everyone has many to recount. Two outstanding ones in my life come to mind. The first helped me to form an identity with my family, and the second with God.

The first took place on Christmas Day when I was five years old. I awoke with mumps that morning, making it impossible for me to attend the big family tree gathering at my Grandparents' home on the adjoining farm. I was permitted, however, to go and peek through the window so I could see my baby cousin who had come from North Carolina for Christmas. What I saw as I peeked through the window was unforgettable. A host of aunts, uncles, and cousins were laughing and talking at the same time while my grandmother sat erectly at the piano playing carols. The tree overflowed into the middle of the room with gifts. But the most impressive sight of all was my grandaddy's tear-streaked face as he watched his beloved daughter and her baby whom he seldom saw. That room was filled with love. It housed my family, and even though I was on the outside looking in, I was very much a part. In that room were the people who loved me most . This was my heritage, and it gave me a rich, warm feeling inside to know that I belonged.

The second experience occurred when I was nine years old. It was a beautiful day in May and school had closed for the summer vacation. I pulled off my shoes and ran through the spring meadow. The pink and blue larkspur were in full bloom and the crimson clover made a soft carpet under my feet. I looked up toward the tall hill that rose to the east and saw the trees in full foliage and each one had a bird singing in it. Feeling the freedom from school, shoes, and routine I turned my face to the sun's warmth and smiled inside and outside. At the top of that hill I could feel God's presence and he seemed to be smiling back at me. He became very real to me that day. Though many years have elapsed and many miles have separated me from that scene, when I pray I sometimes picture God at the top of that hill smiling at me just as he did on that day.

There have been many rich experiences in my adult life such as my wedding day, the birth days of my babies and the happy family gatherings, but the experiences of those early, impressionable years leave their mark on life forever. How richly God nourishes us with happy childhood experiences and poignant memories!

Conclusion

We, as parents, want to provide bountifully for our children and to meet all of their needs. God not only wants to provide but knows our needs and has access to all provisions. He indeed becomes our El Shaddai nourishing us physically, emotionally, and spiritually!

1. Kay Arthur, *Lord, I Want To Know You* (Portland, Oregon: Multnomah Press), p. 27.
2. Charles Allen, *God's Psychiatry* (Old Tappan, New Jersey: Fleming Revel Co., 1953) p.113.
3. Francis Boyd Calhoun, *Miss Minerva and William Green Hill* (MCMLX by Riley and BrittonCo., 1909).
4. Max Lucado, *God Came Near* (Portland, Oregon: Multnomah Press, 1987), p 25. Used by permission.
5. 2 Peter 1:16.

THOUGHTS FOR DISCUSSION

1. Discuss ways in which God provides for our physical needs today and our responsibilities in relation to them.
2. What are some ways God may discipline us today?
3. How does Jesus provide for us as:
   The Author and Perfector of our faith?
   The True Vine?
   The Sacrificial Lamb?
   The Good Shepherd?
   The Way, the Truth, and the Life?
4. Recount experiences God has given you that remain in your heart and mind and nourish you over the years.
5. Discuss the breakdown of the home as God designed it and its effect on the emotional well being of children and adults.
6. How can we, as a church, enhance the emotional stability of those who did not enjoy the blessings of a godly home?
7. Discuss the purpose of church discipline. How can it be used effectively today? How can it be abused?

Prayer Thought: "Thank you for your abundant and overflowing love which nourishes us continually."

Chapter Four

WOMAN: NURTURER OF FAMILY

As God is our El Shaddai, The All Sufficient One, nourishing us physically, emotionally, and spiritually so we, in turn, are to reach out to others. We have been nourished to nourish! Our responsibility to do good is directed toward all men, and we find the avenues of service to be infinite. We, however, are restricted by time and opportunity, so we must plan wisely in order to be most effective. Even Jesus, with complete power, touched only a few lives directly during his lifetime. His thirty two years were spent within a narrow region and he had to be selective.

God gives us certain guidelines to follow in choosing our service. These might be considered a hierarchy of responsibilities. First, we must consider our immediate family.

But if anyone does not provide for his own, and *especially* for those of his own household, he has denied the faith and is worse than an unbeliever. (1 Tim. 5:8)

But if any widow has children or grandchildren, let them first learn to show

piety at home and to repay their parents,
for this is good and acceptable before God.
(1 Tim. 5:4)

Beyond our own families we have responsibilities to all those around us, but fellow Christians get preferential treatment.

Therefore, as we have opportunity, let us
do good to all , *especially* to those who are
of the household of faith. (Gal. 6:10)

Our outreach then, begins at home, extends to the church, and finally to the entire world. We cannot ignore this hierarchy of service without ignoring God.

In keeping with Jesus' teaching concerning priorities in ministry our emphasis in this chapter will be on ways we can nourish members of our own family. Our outreach to others will be considered in the following chapter.

Establish Priorities

We can all see the absurdity of a young mother leaving her baby at home to go on a world mission tour, or leaving her own sick child unattended to do volunteer work at the hospital. But, do we sometimes attempt to justify the neglect of the teaching and training of our own children while taking jobs teaching or training others? We can get so busy reaching out that we fail to reach our own. I believe much of this conflict of interest comes from a misunderstanding of priorities as God sees them.

There are stages in life when the needs of our own family consume us. We have little or nothing left over for others. An infant's needs are overwhelming! God purposefully created babies with constant need for food, changing, burping, fondling and communication. Care of infants was not intended to be a trivial task, and no mother should feel guilty for devoting full time to it.

At the end of a chaotic day spent with her colicky baby my daughter was asked, "Well, what did you do today, Cheryl?" "I just grew McKenna one day older," she replied. A notable task in God's eyes, I feel sure!

God exempted mothers of infants from the annual excursion to Jerusalem for the religious feast. The feast was important, but the baby more so. A mother's first responsibility was to properly nourish her own.

God said, "As we have opportunity do good to all men."[1] This qualifies our service. Accepting the responsibility at home which is mine is often harder than looking for another, more desirable opportunity outside the home.

My husband's grandmother devoted her life to the care of an invalid daughter, so she had little outreach to others. She cheerfully and willingly tended to every need until the daughter had to be permanently hospitalized. At that time Grannie said she could die in peace knowing her work was completed. Will God fault her for the lack of outreach to fellow church members, or of mission efforts which were not opportune for her, when she accepted a much more difficult task, which was hers?

Parents of special children, "physically or mentally challenged," are heavily loaded for life. They may see many opportunities for service away from home, but most of these will have to remain out of reach because the opportunity at hand is all consuming.

Giving our families priority treatment is not always easy. One of the reasons that young mothers are leaving their infants and young children to seek opportunities elsewhere could be due to the overwhelming nature of the work. They, being startled by the constant demands made on their time, seek other, less strenuous opportunites. By not "hanging tough" they may miss the most important opportunity of life, that of personally teaching and training their own.

We, like God, are to nourish physically, emotionally and spiritually. There is a close relationship among these areas and it is hard to separate them. Each hinges on the other. God's physical care portrays his love to us, and our physical care of others demonstrates not only our love for them, but our love for God as well. Though the areas do overlap we will look at each individually.

Nurturing Physically

Physical nourishment is often the most obvious and easiest form of nourishment to supply, but it is by no means insignificant. It takes time, money, willingness to be inconvenienced, energy, and self-denial to minister to others physically. A mother may be overwhelmed with the amount of physical nourishment it takes for her family. Even before a baby is born she begins nourishing him through the umbilical cord, after birth through the breast, and as he matures with a spoon. This provision of food continues until the child is grown. The majority of her time in the home is devoted to meals; shopping, preparing, and cleaning up. Secondly, a large portion goes to physical chores such as laundry, cleaning, mending, and sewing. Her personal time for Bible study and prayer is often limited. She may long for more time to communicate with God, her husband, and children. The question comes to mind, "Why is my time devoted to trivials when I want to concentrate on the more noble aspects of life?"

Perhaps we are underestimating the benefits of physical service. Family meals are becoming a lost tradition, but they can be the highlight of the day. This is often the only activity the entire family engages in, and if family members congregate to share in physical nourishment, they may be nourished emotionally as well. The conversation, the sharing of events of the day, the laughter, the smiles, the hearts turned to God in united thanksgiving are all food for the soul. A wise mother may perceive this to be an opportunity for throwing in an inspirational thought, or triggering a discussion on a pertinent issue. She is surrounded with a captive audience.

The table has always been significant in our home. It was the first piece of furniture we bought. The oval, Early American table looked so large as my husband, my two small daughters, and I took our places around it. In a short time two more daughters were added, filling it to capacity. Then came a son, and the need for a larger table became urgent. My father-in-law built us a table out of a slab of beautiful oak wood. We had great joy in assembling our large family of seven around that table. It seemed only a short time until our family expanded again. Our oldest daughter married, then our second oldest and then our third. They and their mates joined us frequently for meals and our table was again bursting at the seams. Though our budget was limited we gathered all of our accessible cash and bought a large, glass paneled table which comfortably seats ten. It was ultra important to us to provide a table large enough to accommodate our extended family. We have long since filled it and run over the edge, but my most treasured memories are of the times we have gathered around the table and shared our hopes, dreams, and innermost feelings, as well as our daily bread. Still, when those special occasions arise and our large family assembles I look on those surrounding me and thank God I have had a part, though in a small way, in making them who they are simply through supplying their physical needs.

Nurturing Emotionally

There is an interdependency between physical and emotional nourishment. What joy a newlywed wife gets from preparing favorite meals for her husband! Ironing his shirts can be an act of love rather than a chore.

When we had four teenage daughters to dress I spent a lot of time at the sewing machine. Sewing was not an art to me but a necessity. I knew each girl's waist measurement, her bust size, and the imperfections in her bone structure. I thought of her day's activities and the plans that involved the wearing of the new dress as I sewed and it made my work easy. Sewing costumes, banquet dresses, and finally pure white satin wedding dresses endeared each of them to me and gave me a tangible part in their lives. It impressed me that as we render physical services to others, they become endeared to us. Love inspires action and action breeds love. The physical and emotional aspects of ministry are too close to be separated.

There are times when the greatest emotional support we can offer our family is simply our presence. A mother's presence in the home gives security to the entire family. Each may appear to be independent, busy at his or her own project and unaware of her, but if she disappears for a while the household turns into turmoil. Her presence can be profound. It is equally satisfying to the mother to know that her presence is valued. Her baby lights up at the sight of her face and her husband does not relax when he enters the door of his domain until he locates her. As she nourishes her family emotionally, she herself is nourished. We hear a lot about quality time spent with the family, but all time is quality time when it's spent with those we love.

There are times, however, when our presence is not needed. We must respect the right of privacy and the need to sometimes be alone. Some children are more private and demand more solitude than others. There are times when our husbands need space.

Jesus, when grieving over John the Baptist's death, went away to be by himself. The multitude, insensitive and unaware of his need for privacy, descended upon him clamoring for attention. We want to be more aware of our family members' needs and be available, but not intrusive, forcing ourselves into their private domains. God has given each a distinct personality and it becomes my responsibility to guide and nurture without prying into confidences. Recognizing my child to be God's, not my own personal possession, will assist in this area. We need an occasional reminder to *mother*, not *smother*.

A natural response to love is the desire to minister. Those who knew and loved Jesus in person wanted to render a physical service to him. His feet were washed with tears and dried with a woman's hair (Luke 7:38). He was the recipient of a precious gift of perfume. His body was anointed for burial, wrapped in linen, and buried in a gift-tomb by those who loved him (Luke 27:59-60).

Nurturing Spiritually

Our physical ministry is not petty. It is true, however, that we can devote so much of our time to meeting the physical and emotional needs that we may neglect the more important spiritual needs of those around us. Direct teaching and training play an important role and have been touched on in an earlier chapter. However, we also mentor our children in godliness by living our faith before them daily. Deuteronomy 6:4-7 speaks of teaching as we walk, stand, lie down and rise up. In other words, as we go through the ordinary motions of life we are communicating God to them. Our faith is shown by attitude. We may say we are committed to God, but in reality are we more committed to comfort and leisure than to the needs around us? Do we really go out of our way to help others? Is our conversation centered on this world or the next? Are we weighed down with cares which we fail to relinquish to God? As our children grow older do we show preference for them to lead a life of service or a life of worldly success? Are we more excited about good grades than good behavior?

Unless I am fully committed to God I won't be able to mentor my children in godliness. Its not as simple as sending them to Bible class, summer Bible camp or Vacation Bible School. A much broader concept is presented in Deuteronomy which involves walking with God and family in a dual relationship.

One Saturday morning I was in the attic getting down warm fall clothes for my children to wear to church the next day. Two young ladies came to my door carrying Bibles and were met by my children at the door. They ran to the attic excitedly to tell me some women were there to study the Bible. I, occupied with my own plans for the day, told them to tell the young ladies I was too busy this morning. After they were gone my daughters looked very disappointed and one said, "They even had their Bibles with them and wanted to study." I was instantly remorseful and tried to find the young ladies, but it was too late. I had shown my children that I was more concerned with what we would wear than with seeking first the kingdom of God and his righteousness.

Grandparent Involvement

Grandmothers have wonderful opportunities to nurture their grandchildren spiritually. Lois played a vital role in Timothy's training (2 Tim. 1:5). Many caring grandmothers today provide the nurturing their daughters or daughter-in-laws are unable to provide. Even though their energy level is lower and their infatuation with babies has diminished their deep concern for the spiritual well being of their offspring is motivation enough to cause them to over-extend themselves. My grandmother provided untold spiritual encouragement for me. When I was five my granddaddy died. I spent many nights with my grandmother shortly after his death to keep her company. Those times were wonderful faith builders for me. As she faced giving up her home, moving and starting a new job she radiated trust and joy in the Lord. As we lay in the big, high posted bed reciting our favorite verses she confidently spoke Romans 8:38.

> For I am persuaded that neither death nor life, nor angels nor principalities nor angels nor principalities nor powers, nor things present nor things to come, nor height nor depth, nor any other created thing, shall be able to separate us from the love of God which is in Christ Jesus our Lord.

Sleeping in the same bed on which my granddaddy had been prepared for burial a few days earlier, I thought her to be the bravest woman I knew, and I also knew where she got her strength.

Nurturing our Mates

Wives have a great opportunity to nourish their mates spiritually, as well as physically and emotionally. Marriage is a shared experience and a wife is certainly to exert her influence to persuade him toward service, selflessness, and humility. Think of the marriage traumas that could have been reversed had these wives used their influence on their husbands for good rather than evil: Adam and Eve, Ahab and Jezebel, Annanias and Sapphira, Haman and Zeresh. It was Eve who suggested tasting the forbidden fruit (Gen. 3:6), Jezebel who seized the coveted vineyard (1 Kings 21:17), Sapphira who agreed with her husband to lie to God (Acts 5:2), and Zeresh who advocated a scaffold for Mordacai (Es. 5:14).

Marriage is a partnership, a unified effort, which most often stands or falls as one. How great to be a part of a married team which is known for its united effort for good such as Abraham and Sarah, Isaac and Rebecca, Joseph and Mary, Zacharias and Elizabeth, and Acquilla and Priscilla!

My mother is a great example of a godly wife. When she married my daddy she knew him to be well traveled, knowledgeable in the Bible, a good conversationalist and well informed on many subjects, but she did not know until after she was married that he had anxiety disorders which caused emotional and mental problems. He was the thirteenth child in his family, and of necessity received little attention at home. His participation in World War I had also left emotional scars. For days at a time he sat picking a banjo and staring out the window. When I was old enough to realize what a difficult marriage this must have been I asked if it didn't scare her when she realized what lay ahead. "No," she replied. "I just knew I would devote my life to helping him go to Heaven." And that is what she did. Sixty seven years of marriage were devoted to loving, honoring and inspiring him while he steadily grew and developed into the man God created him to be. He was beloved by all who knew him, exerting a strong influence in the home, the church, and the community. He taught Bible classes and served as an elder in the church. He had a great love for children and he knew the name of each child in the congregation. He always carried a *goodie bag* in his pocket to pass out to the children when worship was over, showing that their presence was important. This small gesture of kindness had more impact on the congregation than we knew until the time of his death. A large candy wreath composed of lollipops, candy canes, and goodies was sent with a card signed from the children of the community, past and present.

The last six weeks of Daddy's life were spent in a Veteran's hospital fighting a painful battle against cancer. Cards arrived after his death from the doctors and nurses at the Veteran's hospital, marveling at the patience, humor and faith he exhibited during that trying ordeal. As one doctor said, "Your daddy had a remarkable philosophy of life." This was because God reigned in his heart.

In his old age he praised my mother for being the one person most responsible for his salvation and often thanked God for sending her into his life. My mother viewed marriage much as Queen Esther's queenship was viewed, "Who knows whether you have come to the kingdom for such a time as this?" (Es. 4:14).

In considering my daddy's life of Christian growth and maturity, the question comes to mind, how did my mother have such a profound influence on him? She never nagged, never criticized, never warned. She was always kind, patient, and positive. She put God first in her own life even when it meant walking the two miles to church in the snow, or giving to the Lord the little bit of money she saved from selling eggs, money which she needed so badly for household supplies. She read the Bible aloud to the family each evening, and my daddy enjoyed it as much as anyone. He got excited over the Old Testament characters and prophecies and committed long passages to memory from both Old and New Testaments. Her love for him and especially for his soul was forefront in all she did. He was lovingly nurtured into a relationship with God which sustained him through some trying times. As he lay on his death bed for the sixth week without being able to swallow a bite of food or a drop of water he prayed aloud each night thanking God for his constant presence and entreating God to take him to be with him soon.

Conclusion

Nurturing members of our own families may be the greatest work we will ever be privileged to experience. What joy could equal that of knowing we had a part in the eternal salvation of our spouses, children, or grandchildren?

How sweet, how heav'nly, is the sight,
When those that love the Lord
In one another's peace delight,
And so fulfill the word.[2]

1. Galations 6:10.
2. E. L. Jorgenson, *Great Songs of the Church* (Rand Mcnally and Co., 1974), p.400.

THOUGHTS FOR DISCUSSION

1. Discuss ways to make family devotionals appealing to children of varying ages.
2. When family meals cannot be arranged what substitute can be worked out for family assembly?
3. Does placing our children first make them self centered or more willing to serve others unselfishly?
4. How can we allow for and respect solitude if our space is limited and children must share rooms?
5. Husbands and wives influence each other for bad or good. What steps can be taken to ensure that it be for good?

Prayer Thought: " May I nourish my family lavishly and lovingly as you continually nourish me."

Chapter Five

WOMAN: NURTURER OF ALL

Now may He who supplies seed to the
sower and bread for food, supply and
multiply the seed you have sown and
increase the fruits of your righteousness.
While you are enriched in everything for all
liberality, which causes thanksgiving
through us to God. (2 Cor. 9:10-11)

While our family's needs take precedence over all
others, we can learn a valuable lesson from the noble
wife who was described in Proverbs. She was tireless
in her efforts to feed, clothe and shelter her own family,
but she also found time to reach out to the poor. If we
are open to opportunity we, too, will find ways to serve
those outside our family unit, ministering to them
physically, emotionally, and spiritually. James reminds
us that pure religion is looking after orphans and widows
in their distress as well as keeping ourselves unpolluted
by the world (James I:27).

Importance of Nurturing

Our response to others is significant because it places us on his right hand with the sheep, or on his left with the goats. A judgment scene is pictured in Matthew 25:32-40. We hear Jesus speak to the sheep:

'Come, you who are blessed of My Father;
inherit the kingdom prepared for you from
the foundation of the world! For I was
hungry and you gave Me food . I was thirsty
and you gave Me drink; I was a stranger
and you took Me in, I was naked and you
clothed Me, I was sick and you visited me, I
was in prison and you came to Me.'

These are simple acts which hold eternal significance. Those saved were saved because they responded to the needs of others while those lost simply were unaware. Awareness carries with it responsibility, and responsibility calls for action.

Our response to others is, in a sense, our response to Christ. "Assuredly, I say to you, inasmuch as you did it to one of the least of these My brethren, you did it to Me" (Matt. 25:40).

For he who does not love his brother whom
he has seen, how can he love God, whom
he has not seen?..And this commandment
we have from Him: that he who loves God
must love his brother also. (1John 4:20-21)

It is more difficult to love our fellow man who is filled with imperfections and who conflicts with us and our will than to love our unseen, perfect creator who, himself, is love. Yet, love for our fellow man is the true test of our love for God.

I heard a little poem once, which describes this dilemma well.

To live above with saints we love
Oh! That will be the glory.
To live below with saints we know
Now that's a different story!

Love for our fellow man is given equal place with self-love by Christ. The royal command states, "Love your neighbor as yourself,"[1] self-love being assumed. "After all, no one ever hated his own flest, but nourishes and cherishes it, just as the Lord does the church" (Eph. 5:29).

Assuming that I possess a natural talent for loving myself it behooves me to take God's admonitions seriously and to look introspectively.

Look to yourselves (Gal. 6:1)RSV

Examine yourself. (2 Cor. 13:5)

First remove the plank from your own eye, and then you will see clearly to remove the speck out of your brother's eye. (Matt. 7:5)

Surely, upon close examination, I will recognize myself to be one of the unlovely people God saw fit to love. Having looked inward and upward I will be better equipped to look outward, to be more tolerant of my unlovely neighbor, and to consider his needs as important as mine.

Who is My Neighbor?

If my salvation depends on my love for my neighbor it becomes urgent to know who that person is. I, like the lawyer who asked Jesus this question, may ask, attempting to limit, restrict, or confine in order to fit him into my small realm of fellowship.

Jesus, on the other hand, took the narrow Jewish concept of neighbor which meant one with whom one lives in a reciprocal relationship, and broadened it. He removed all boundaries and limitations, making it an all inclusive term for any fellow human being who is in need.

There are many we would like to eliminate from our do-good list: the tactless, the social misfits, the complainers, the unappreciative and the depressed. To do so would mean we were determining our benevolence on grounds of personality rather than need. Jesus stripped the term neighbor bare, leaving only a colorless, unknown human being, even one of the "least of these."

Flexibility

Accepting opportunity to be wherever need is found involves flexibility, the willingness to turn aside from our own plans to minister to a more pressing need. This is very difficult for most of us. We become so engrossed with our own schedules we scarcely leave time for the unplanned and the spontaneous. It is good to be active, and to form a plan, but we also must develop a wise passiveness in which we remain open to whatever change must be made to meet more urgent needs.

Jesus can be noted as one who was willing and able to lay aside his own plan to meet a more pressing need. He turned aside from his ministry of men to minister to little children. The disciples saw them only as an interruption, but Jesus welcomed them as an opportunity.

Jesus ignored his own need for solitude after John the Baptist's death to nourish a multitude of men who were clamoring for his attention (Matt. 14:10-14). Situations which would be perceived as hindrances to most were considered as opportunities by Jesus.

Mary was commended by Jesus for acting on the opportunity of the day when she anointed his feet with precious perfume (Mark 14:3). Her gift was worth a year's wages. Perhaps she had pondered and planned what would be the best use of her money. If so, she quickly set aside her plan to seize a greater opportunity, that of serving her Lord. She can be hailed as an opportunist for her timely gift.

Instead of making our own rigid plans, "Today or tomorrow I will go to this or that city,"[2] and seeking opportunities which are not timely or appropriate we want God to make the opportunity of the day obvious to us. If we act on it, then God's plan will be expedited and his work accomplished.

Hospitality

Openness to opportunity is characterized by an attitude of genuine hospitality. This implies an attitude of solicitude toward guests. It means taking people in at their convenience, not mine. It involves meeting their needs in their time frame. This is more than preparing a nice meal when my house is immaculate and inviting in guests of my choice.

My grandparents had an open-door policy. Anyone was welcome at any time. Company came often and uninvited. They never knew who would be going home with them from church servicesuntil they got there. There were numerous widows who came for several days at a time and elderly aunts and uncles who "dropped in" for rather lengthy stays. I heard it said that when a certain large family drove up in their buggy my grandmother headed straight for the chicken yard to dress chickens for dinner. It was not simple to prepare a meal at her house. She started a fire in the wood stove, picked and broke beans from the garden, killed and dressed her meat, made cake from scratch, then brought water from the spring to wash dishes. It was a full day's work and involved the entire family. Yet, the fellowship was wonderful and everyone was blessed by it.

My parents' home was the same. Their house was always open to anyone who wanted to visit; for a day, a weekend, or a week. Cousins came from the city in the summer because they needed the experiences offered on the farm. Two children, whose parents divorced, spent a summer with my parents because they had no other place to go and were loved and well cared for there. Often a frightened widow who lived across the hill came about dusk for a "little visit" and ended up spending the night. A fresh gown was furnished and clean sheets provided and I never heard a complaint from my parents. A family of sharecroppers who could not read nor write lived on the adjoining farm for many years, and came daily to have their mail read, orders filled out, or telephoning done. They were always treated cordially.

Today's world is filled with modern conveniences, including self-cleaning electric ovens, microwaves, freezers, food mixes of every description, ice makers and dishwashers. Yet, too often we are stingy when it comes to showing hospitality. We consider our time our own, our homes our personal property to be shared only at our convenience. Our dens become just that, hideouts from our neighbor. The front porch which was once a welcome mat of hospitality is now merely decorative in nature. Is our generation more selfish? Or perhaps less concerned? It could be that we are perfectionists, thinking only a splendid dinner and spotless house fitting for our guests.

Fellowship is no less pleasant when sharing a simple meal, and the relaxed attitude of the hostess is always appreciated. There are easy ways to prepare for the unexpected, such as having a frozen casserole on hand with an easy salad and dessert stowed away. I know one lady who keeps a sack with her "emergency meal" in her cabinet at all times containing cans for an easy, complete dinner that can be concocted in five minutes. The willingness to simplify can expedite genuine hospitality.

The ministry of showing hospitality to others is stressed by God. Romans 12:13 admonishes us to practice hospitality. 1 Timothy 5:10, and 1 Peter 4:9 also teach the importance of opening our homes to others. We are given remarkable examples of women in the Bible who made great sacrifice to show hospitality. The widow of Zarapheth gave her last bite of bread to a stranger, not knowing there would be any more food for her son or herself (1 Kings 17:10-15). The Shunamite woman was certainly not grudging in showing hospitality to Elisha, a frequent guest, but added a spare room on her house to show her sincere delight in his visits (2 Kings 4:9-10). Sarah also baked bread and prepared a meal for strangers who were later revealed to be angels.

Timeliness

Openness to opportunity involves timeliness. What is appropriate today may not necessarily be timely tomorrow. An elderly person is lonesome, needing someone with whom to share an afternoon of pleasantries. Right now, however, I haven't an afternoon to spend. Later, when I have lots of afternoons to reminisce there is no one who needs to share those memories.

Neighbors are having a family crisis. I plan to get involved...later. Then they drive away, part of the family and belongings going one direction, and part another.

The remorse of a missed opportunity is heavy. I know. I've experienced it many times. One thing is sure, though. That particular opportunity will never reoccur, and trying to recapture it may only bring on problems. Realizing we have not been as involved or aware of needs as we should have been, we overwhelm them with attention which is showered on them too late. They no longer need our deluge of attention. Our untimely efforts may create friction. Dwelling needlessly on missed opportunities will only blind me to the opportunity of the day. God warded off this tendency with the admonition: "As you have opportunity" (Gal. 6:10).

Get Involved

A friend made a comment in Bible class which has been helpful to me. She said that instead of waiting to do the big deed she was always planning to do in event of death or illness, she had found it was better to do the small thing, whatever it was, today. Then, if there was more money or time available later she could still act on her best plan. A call made or a card sent is preferable to a meal planned but never prepared. It is not the bigness of the act that counts, but the fact that you acted.

Physical nourishment is important, but emotional even more so. Though I "give all I possess to feed the poor and surrender my body to the flames, but have not love, I am nothing," says Paul.[3]

Involvement in the lives of people was both practiced and taught by Jesus. In this way he nourished them emotionally. Before we can offer much in the time of crisis or need we must have formed a bond of friendship. It is hard to minister to one with whom we have no rapport, and our overtures of kindness may be rejected if offered only in emergencies. Jesus was involved in the lives of Mary and Martha before Lazarus died or he wouldn't have been able to weep with them in their sorrow (John 11:5-6). They would not have sent for him in their crisis.

Ministering emotionally often means simply offering our presence. Not knowing what to say or do does not excuse us from going to the grieved, the lonely, those with marriage problems, the terminally ill, the woman who has miscarried, the girl who has conceived out of wedlock, the couple who has found they cannot have children. Simply being there counts. "Better is a neighbor who is near than a brother who is far away" (Prov 27:10). Ruth had little to offer Naomi in her emptiness, but the promise of her continual presence was enough to sustain her.

There are times, however, when our presence is not needed. We must respect the right of privacy and the need to sometimes be alone. Solomon gave some advice concerning this. "Seldom set foot in your neighbor's house, lest he become weary of you and hate you" (Prov. 25:17).

Knowing when to be present and when not requires understanding. A little more solitude is needed by some than others. If we are very sensitive to needs we will know when that time is and will slip quietly away.

Show Acceptance

Solomon gave another bit of advice concerning emotional nourishment: accept others as they are. Neither tear them down by belittlement, nor build them up unduly by flattery. "A man who flatters his neighbor spreads a net for his feet" (Prov 29:5).

Jesus was able to minister to lepers, social outcasts, sinners, a short man in a tree, a woman with a tainted past as well as a host of other unlovely people simply because his attitude toward them was one of acceptance. He saw them as God's creations, people worth dying for.

It has been said that we love, not because of how we feel about a person, but rather how that person makes us feel about ourselves. Acceptance is vital to the emotional well-being of others.

Edify

Spiritual edification climaxes our outreach to others. "If in this life only we have hope, we are of all men the most pitiable" (1 Cor. 15:19).

We often miss the opportunity to minister spiritually because we have neglected the physical and emotional needs. Spiritual edification is sometimes an outgrowth of physical and emotional ministry. It is hard to convince one of the joy of Christian fellowship if he or she has suffered pain or grief and no one has offered comfort, or if no one has been there to rejoice in the times of triumph.

A neighbor was approached about letting her child go to church but she emphatically said, "No." She told how the members of that church had excluded her child from play, had been inhospitable to her and her children, and were only interested in getting a bigger head count at church. Whether true or not, it was her perception. It is hard sometimes to minister spiritually unless we have first ministered to the physical and emotional needs.

My grandmother had a spiritual influence on many in the community in which she lived. Most of her influence, I believe, could be accredited to the fact that she was neighborly. She found many ways to minister to physical needs. In her old age I asked her how many births she assisted and she counted 32 babies on whom she had pinned the first diaper, not in an official capacity but rather as a friend. She always invited, exhorted, and admonished spiritually as naturally as she ministered physically. I learned from her what it means to care and to keep on caring for a neighbor's soul even when that person no longer wants that concern. Grandmother's friend and neighbor, Mrs. Pearl, lived nearby. Even though her grown children were Christians she had never accepted Christ. Periodically, Grandmother called Mrs. Pearl to invite her to church, but she always declined. One day she replied resolutely, "No, Lillian. I'm not interested so don't bother me again." Grandmother hung the phone up sadly, not because she had been rebuked, but because of her concern for her friend.

I knew my grandmother well enough to know she wasn't through. A few months later our gospel meeting was starting and I was helping Mother prepare a big dinner when Grandmother posed an idea, as if it were brand new. "I think I'll invite Pearl to dinner and to the meeting." Even Mother looked hesitant, but Grandmother had another strategy. I eavesdropped on her phone call and heard her say, "Pearl, I was just thinking about how much we've shared in life. We use to court in the same buggy. We married on the same day. We have witnessed the births of 12 children between us. I do so wish we were going to Heaven together. Won't you come to our meeting and hear the good preaching and eat dinner with us?" I knew, even before I heard the reply that she couldn't resist that invitation. Sure enough! She said she would. I witnessed her baptism in the little creek in front of the church that afternoon, and I saw her hobble into church every Sunday thereafter, even when she had to come with a walker.

Conclusion

Grandmother was a living testimony to me that we can never quit caring for our neighbors, either physically, emotionally, or spiritually. We may become discouraged. We may experience fatigue and disheartenment, but we cannot afford to quit. The soul of a friend is too valuable!

Lord, speak to me that I may speak
In living echoes of Thy tone;
As Thou has sought, so let me seek
Thine erring children, lost and lone.

O strengthen me, that while I stand
Firm on the Rock and strong in Thee,
I may stretch out a loving hand
To wrestlers with the troubled sea.

O teach me Lord, that I may teach
The precious things Thou dost impart;
And wing my words that they may reach
The hidden depths of many a heart.

O fill me with Thy fullness, Lord
Until my very heart o'er-flow;
In kindling tho't and glowing word,
Thy love to tell, Thy praise to show.[4]

1. Mark 12:23.
2. James 4:3.
3. 1 Corinthians 13:3.
4. E. L. Jorgenson, *Great Songs of the Church* (Rand Mcnally and Co., 1974), p. 438.

THOUGHTS FOR DISCUSSION

1. What can we do to reach out to the unlovely - those who most need love?
2. How can we become more comfortable with ministering to those who are ill or grieving, especially grief over something other than death?
3. Discuss ways of ministering to those with whom we come in contact without spending a day preparing.
4. What role does physical nourishment play in setting the scene for spiritual nourishment?
5. Are there risks for us when we reach out to the unlovely? If so, what are they?

Prayer Thought: " O Lord, help me not to overlook the magnitude of hurting people in the world around me. Let me reach out to them as you have reached out to me."

WORKING

Chapter Six

GOD OF INDUSTRY

God is the epitome of power to accomplish. The
Bible begins with an account of his work week, and what
a fruitful week it was! The vastness of his works is noted
by David.

O Lord, how manifold are Your works! In
wisdom You have made them all. The earth
is full of Your possessions. This great and
wide sea in which are innumerable
teeming things, living things both great and
small...These all wait for You that You may
give them their food in due season...May
the glory of the Lord endure forever; may
the Lord rejoice in his works. (Psa.104: 24,
25, 27, 31)

The significance of God's works lies, not in their
own greatness, but in their ability to point to his
greatness thereby bringing glory to him.

The heavens declare the glory of God and
the firmament shows His handiwork. Day
unto day utters speech, And night unto

night reveals knowledge. There is no speech nor language where their voice is not heard. (Psa. I9:1-3)

How awesome are Your works! Through the greatness of Your power Your enemies should submit themselves to You...Come and see the works of God. (Psa.66:3, 5, 6)

God's Works are Faith Builders

God's works have served as faith builders through all ages. The father of a demon-filled son acknowledged Jesus as "Teacher," but admitted to having a small faith. After seeing Jesus cast the demon out of his son that seed of faith grew into amazement (Mark 9:I3). Peter, recognizing Christ to be Lord, agreed to move the nets into deep water if Jesus advised, even though they had fished all night to no avail. Upon seeing the enormity of Christ's miracle of fish, Peter responded with a greater faith than ever before: "Depart from me for I am a sinful man, O Lord!" (Luke 5:8). Thomas, a doubting follower, witnessed the resurrected Christ and confessed, "My Lord, and my God!" (John 20:28).

Even where faith is non-existent the works of God can ignite it. After having witnessed Daniel's triumph in the lions' den King Darius sent a letter regarding Daniel's God.

I make a decree that in every dominion of my kingdom men must tremble and fear before the God of Daniel...He delivers and he works signs and wonders in heaven and on earth. Who has delivered Daniel from the power of the lions. (Dan. 6:26-27)

The centurion soldier who was guarding Jesus

saw the earthquake and exclaimed, "Surely he was the Son of God!" (Luke 23:47)KJV. Those present when the widow of Nain's son was raised from the dead were filled with awe, praised God and said, "God has visited his people" (Luke 7:16).

These are only a few examples of faith being increased by a new perception of God's greatness evidenced through his works. The stories of his past works, as well as his ongoing works, continue to act as faith cinchers for all of us. They are as awe-inspiring today as ever.

God's Works are in His Control

God's works, while great, are always controlled by him. He has charge over them, not they over him. Though set up to perform in one way he has often over-ridden their natural course, and worked in a way suitable for his particular purpose. The sea rolled back and congealed in order to accommodate the children of Israel. The rain ceased in behalf of Elijah's prayer. God breathed fire on a bush which did not consume it. He made dumb animals talk, reversed the sundial, and caused the sun to stand still.

God allowed Elijah to survey a variety of his handiwork from the mountain, showing that while he controls mountain-shattering winds, earthquakes, and fire, he can also manifest his glory through a still, gentle whisper (1 Kings l9:12).

In keeping with his father's control over creation Jesus showed himself also to be Lord of all nature. He walked on water, calmed the storm with a command, cured uncurable diseases and triumphed over death. Laws of nature had been decreed by him, and therefore could easily be changed by him. He still maintains control.

We, being part of his works, are also in his control. Job came to realize this through a series of hard questions asked by God:

Where were you when I laid the foundations of the earth?
Have you commanded the morning since your days began,, and caused the dawn to know its place?
Have you entered the springs of the sea, or have you walked in search of the depths?
Have you comprehended the breadth of the earth?
Do you know the ordinances of the heavens? Can you set their dominion over the earth?
Have you an arm like God?, Or can you thunder with a voice like his? (Job 38:4, 12, 16, 18, 33, Job 40:9)

Having contemplated the works of God Job responded by saying, "I know that You can do everything; and that no purpose of Yours can be withheld from You. Therefore, I have uttered what I did not understand, things too wonderful for me which I did not know" (Job 42:2-3). Job realized through this endeavor that God's works are unfathomable in the lives of men just as they are in nature. We, being part of his creation, are under his control.

This is contrary to what we would like to believe. Pride wants us to think that we are in control of our lives. "I am the master of my fate. I am the captain of my soul," is the propoganda being fed to me by Satan. It was the philosophy which prevailed during the building of the tower of Babel: "Let us make a name for ourselves"

(Gen. 11:4). God, however, confounded their language to demonstrate to the people that he was in control, not they.

Work is Good

God's attitude toward work is one of satisfaction. The creation, resulting from each day of his work week was pronounced good (Gen. 1). Knowing the joy of accomplishment, God's first command to his children was, "Be fruitful" (Gen. 9:1). He knew that man's happiness was to be found in tending the garden, subduing the earth and multiplying his own seed. Had he been given no garden to tend, no fruit to harvest, nothing to strive for, would he have been happy? It is doubtful. Work was never intended as punishment. When sin entered the picture, painful annoyances were given to afflict their work. It was Satan who tainted an aspect of life which was created for happiness. To the man God said,

Cursed is the ground for your sake; in toil you shall eat of it all the days of your life. Both thorns and thistles it shall bring forth for you, And you shall eat the herb of the field...In the sweat of your face you shall eat bread till you return to the ground (Gen. 3:17-19).

And to woman he said, "I will greatly multiply your sorrow and your conception; In pain you shall bring forth children" (Gen. 3:16).

Hindrances were added, but productivity was not taken away. It was never God's will that we live unfruitful lives. Jesus cursed a non-productive fruit tree. If barrenness was contemptible in a fig tree does he not expect us to lead fruitful lives? God decreed that a man who would not work should not be allowed to eat (2 Thess. 3:10). Work is commanded. We are admonished to mind our own business and work with our hands (1 Thess. 4:11). Work was instigated for our well-being, not for our salvation. Salvation does not hinge on output. God saves. Lazarus, a non-productive beggar, is pictured cradled in Abraham's bosom. The thief on the cross had no opportunity to produce works in keeping with his faith, yet Jesus promised him salvation. It may seem strange to us that the kingdom of God is made up of little children and those who become like them, since children are our least productive (work oriented) citizens --yet safe. Why? Because salvation is God's gift to man.

Milton, in his sonnet, **On His Blindness,** expressed it like this:

God doth not need either man's work or his
own gifts
Who best bear his mild yoke, they serve
him best.
His state is kingly: thousands at his bidding
speed,
and post o'er land and ocean without rest;
They also serve who only stand and wait.[1]

This principle is demonstrated in God's care of the flowers and birds which neither sow, reap, nor labor, yet are cared for abundantly.

Work, then, is God's gift to man, not man's gift to God, and should be accepted with gratitude. Solomon, in speaking of work satisfaction said, "There is nothing better for a man than that he should eat and drink, and that his soul should enjoy good in his labor. This also I saw was from the hand of God" (Eccle. 2:24-25).

Work Expectations are Individual

God's expectations for our productivity are congruent with the talents given. To whom much is given much will be expected. We can be glad productivity is not measured by quantity, but is proportionate to potential. God uses individual measuring sticks. The parable of the talents gives evidence to this (Matt. 25:14-30). Production was rewarded. It was not, however, rewarded according to amount, but according to potential. The man who gained five talents was rewarded equally with the man who gained ten. Only the non-productive was punished. The man given only one talent could have produced only one and been acceptable, but since he was given little he remained status quo. Therefore, he was found displeasing to God.

Idleness Condemned

Effort then is rewarded and idleness condemned by God. He is not idle, nor does he tolerate it in his children. Jesus said, "My father is always at his work even to this day, and I am working" (John 5:17).

Many warnings were given regarding idleness.
The way of a slothful man is like a hedge of thorns. (Prov. 15:19)

The soul of the sluggard desires and has nothing: but the soul of the diligent shall be made rich. (Prov. 13:4-6)

Do not love sleep, lest you come to poverty. (Prov.20:13)

Nor did we eat anyone's bread free of

charge, but worked with labor and toil night and day, that we might not be a burden to any of you. (2 Thes. 3:8)

If anyone will not work, neither shall he eat. (2 Thes. 3:10)

But refuse the younger widows; for when they have begun to grow wanton against Christ, they desire to marry, having condemnation because they have cast off their first faith. And besides they learn to be idle, wandering about from house to house, and not only idle but also gossips and busybodies, saying things which they ought not. (1 Tim. 5:11, 13)

Rest is Good

Idleness is not, however, to be confused with rest. God mixed work with rest. He knew when to work and when not to. We are not always so wise. He valued rest so much that he set aside one of the seven week days for it. This was time allotted for taking pleasure in his new creations. This was the day of unhurried quietude, of repose. Without this interlude of rest we would know him as an ever busy God who valued the product only for the producing of it. We would know nothing of the balance of his nature, of his stillness, or his relaxation coupled with his abundant, overflowing work potential.

Jesus, both man and God, loathed idleness, but practiced rest. He spent quiet time in the mountain. He prayed for hours in the garden. His mission was to "work the works of Him who sent me" (John 9:4), and he knew that the most effective work was that interspersed with rest. When the crowds overwhelmed him and his work closed in he said, "Come aside by yourselves to a deserted place and rest a while" (Mark 6:31). This was not an effort to avoid the people's needs but rather an effort to be more efficient in meeting them.

God recognizes man's need for rest also. Work alone will not suffice. God was aware of this when he gave a law for his people to follow which included a day of rest. If he indulged in a period of rest he certainly expected man to profit from the same.

Once Elijah was overcome with fear and despondency, so he went a day's journey into the desert, sat down under a tree, and prayed to die. "I have had enough, Lord," he said. "Take my life; I am no better than my ancestors." Recognizing Elijah's fatigue, God sent an angel to touch him and to feed him. After Elijah was refreshed with sleep, food and a special measure of God's presence he was able to continue his work with renewed zeal (1 Kings 19:4-6).

Though God has not mandated a Sabbath rest today, the same principle exists. Effective work is not over-work, but work coupled with rest. Surely we need the still and quiet for refreshment and refueling.

Prioritizing Tasks

Jesus not only knew when to work, but he also used wisdom in selecting the right work at the right time. His basis for prioritizing tasks was his father's will. "For I have come down from heaven not to do My own will but to do the will of Him who sent me"(John 6:38). His decisions were never based on selfishness, nor desire.

At the young age of twelve he knew that his responsibility was to be about his father's business. Other tasks would have received precedence by most twelve year old boys, but Jesus learned at an early age to concede to the father.

His next eighteen years were spent in the carpenter's shop. Working as an apprentice to Joseph, he learned the constancy and diligence needed in his trade. During these hours he had time to contemplate the difficult task God had assigned him and to develop the perseverance necessary to complete the task. His hands became calloused and strong, his heart was yielded, his ears attuned to God.

At the age of about thirty years old he left the carpenter's shop, an honorable, safe trade for which he was well trained, to devote himself to a spiritual ministry. Embarking on this ministry meant giving up security of home, family, material possessions, and eventually, life itself. If he had based his decision on selfish desire he would have stayed with his building business. "After all somebody has to do carpentry work," he could have rationalized. Jesus, however, stayed open-minded, always seeking his Father's will. This meant sometimes turning aside from a seemingly important task, to a trivial one. The disciples tried to keep him "on task." They rebuked those who were diverting his attention by bringing little children for blessings. Again, Jesus, in tune with his Father's will, turned aside from his ministry of men to minister to those little ones, "..do not forbid them, for of such is the kingdom of heaven" (Matt. 19:14). He was constantly reevaluating. He was constantly listening to God.

He taught others to prioritize their work also. Martha was working, but she was not doing the most important work at that time. She was aware of her guest and was taking care of his physical needs, but Jesus saw an even more important job to be done and called her attention to it. Disciples were called away from their business of fishing for fish to that of fishing for men. This was a more pressing need.

Conclusion

When we look at Jesus' life we do not see a life filled with *busyness* but with the Father's *business*. We see in him the ability to turn aside from any work if a more important one presented itself. We see an open mind, a searching mind continually seeking the Father's will. His continual mission was to "work the works of him who sent me" (John 9:4).

Even when called to work under the most strenuous conditions, to face opposition, rejection and death on the cross, he persevered to the end, culminating his God-given work with these words, "It is finished."[2]

1. John Milton, "On His Blindness," *Best Loved Poems To Read Again and Again* (New York, New York: Galahad Books, 1986), p.165.
2. John 19:30.

THOUGHTS FOR DISCUSSION

I. Why did God rest on the seventh day since he has inexhaustible strength and never tires?

2. If the Sabbath was mandatory under the Old Law and was established for man's good why was a day of rest not mandated under the new?

3. Can recreation become work and work recreation? If so, how?

4. Will Heaven be a place of rest, void of work? Support your belief with scripture. Read Heb. 3:11, 4:10, and Rev. 14:13 regarding this.

5. Does our society place more value on work which is financially profitable or on work which is service oriented? Jesus engaged in both types. For which was he best known?

Prayer Thought: "Thank you for setting the example of a balanced life. Help us to imitate you in rest as well as in work."

Chapter Seven

THE WORKING WOMAN

> For we are His workmanship, created in
> Christ Jesus for good works, which God
> prepared beforehand that we should walk
> in them (Eph. 2:10).

As a reflector of God's image, work, for me, is not optional, but compulsory. It was part of God's original plan, and was created for my happiness and well-being. My work incentive is to please God, to follow Jesus' precept of "working the works of him who sent me" (John 9:4).

Working Women Cited as Example

When God chose women to cite as examples for us he did not choose vain or idle women, but he chose instead energetic, strong, working women, women with initiative to start difficult works and fortitude to complete them.

The noble woman described by Solomon in Proverbs was noted for her strong arms, eager hands, and business sense. Through her good works she blessed the poor and needy as well as her own household. These works brought her praise at the city gate.

Rebecca, a wife chosen by God for Isaac, was selected perhaps because of her willingness to volunteer for a hard, menial task. Imagine the energy required to replenish water in all those tired, thirsty camels' pouches! Elliezer stood watching, admiring her willingness to serve even a stranger's beasts. No wonder God chose her for the wife of a patriarch! (Gen. 24:46)

And consider Miriam, a faithful, trustworthy babysitter. She helped to spare the child who delivered Israel from bondage (Ex. 2:4).

Deborah, a multitalented, liberated woman of her day, served as wife, prophetess, counselor and judge. As a fearless leader she helped to deliver Israel from the enemy (Jud. 4:4-16).

Working beside Aquilla in the tentmaking industry was his wife, Priscilla. She was also keeping house for a church, and serving as teacher and co-laborer with Paul (Acts 18:2-3, 26, Rom 16:3, 4, 5).

Let us not forget Dorcas who was full of good works and almsdeeds (Acts 9:39-40), or Ruth, a harvester of grain (Ruth 2:2-3).

The Queen of Sheba is an example of one who was so diligent at her business of ruling that she traveled between 1200 and 2000 miles by camel merely to be informed (Acts 10:1-10).

Work, then, is honorable in women, and failure to work is condemned. Paul told the Thessalonians not to feed a person who would not work.[1] A widow's credentials for receiving support from the church included her past involvement in good works, of having brought up children, shown hospitality, helped those in trouble and devoted herself to other good deeds.[2] Pure religion is defined by James as a religion of works including the care of orphans and widows. He also reminds us to be doers of the word and not only hearers, for it is through works that our faith is manifested.[3]

The fate of the non-productive is unpleasant. "And even now the ax is laid at the root of the trees. Therefore every tree which does not bear good fruit is cut down and thrown into the fire" (Luke 3:9).

Discerning God's Will

It is not only important that I work, but that my work be in tune with God's will. Work of my own choosing, that not approved of by God, is doomed to failure from the start.

Unless the Lord builds the house, they
labor in vain.who build it. Unless the Lord
guards the city, the watchmen stays awake
in vain. It is vain for you to rise up early, to
sit up late, to eat the bread of sorrows; - for
so He gives His beloved sleep.
(Psa.127:1-2)

When we devise our own workplans, without consulting God, and without seeking his will we are treading on treacherous ground.

The tower of Babel gave every indication of being a success. The people were united in one effort with common motivation and expectation. Yet, the effort failed because God's blessing was not there.

Sarah strove to help God fulfill his promise to give Abraham a son. She engineered a plan whereby a handmaid was given to Abraham to conceive this son of promise, but God's original plan was not thwarted.

He delivered Isaac as predicted and Sarah's second-guess idea proved to be less than best.

The rich man had a plan, a good work plan. His produce was abundant, and he needed more space to store his goods. "I'll tear down my barns and build up bigger ones, and there I will store all my grain and my goods."[4] But God had a different plan. He was deemed a fool, and his life was taken that very night.

We do not want our work to be in vain, so we must ask for wisdom to discern God's will for our work. "Commit to the Lord whatever you do, and your plans will succeed" (Prov. 16:13).

There are certain works that God has assigned to all of us who are his daughters. Some of these are non-paying, service jobs that involve the general public.

Do not forget to entertain strangers, for by so doing some have unwittingly entertained angels. (Heb. 13:2)

Remember those in prison as if chained with them and those who are mistreated since you yourselves are in the body also. (Heb. 13:3)

The older women are also assigned church work which is appropriate for them.

the older women likewise, that they be reverent in behavior, not slanderers, not given to much wine, teachers of good things - that they admonish the younger women to love their husbands, to love their children, to be discreet, chaste, homemakers, good, obedient to their own husbands, that the word of God may not be blasphemed. (Tit. 2:3-5)

85

These areas of service often go begging because we fill our lives so full of work which is remunerated with pay that we have little time left for free services. Lack of time, however, is not an excuse. Time is the only thing equal in this world, and we are all equally responsible for its use (Eph. 5:16).

Discerning God's will for my work may involve saying "no" to some good works. Martha was one who worked at a commendable task, that of serving her Lord physically by preparing his meal, yet she was not commended by him. What was her problem? Timing. She chose a good work at the wrong time. A spiritual task was available to her and should have taken precedence. A mother of small children may desire to further her education or pursue her career. Her ambitions may be good, but untimely.

Preparation is Work

Sometimes our best work is that of preparation. Young people often get anxious to take on adult responsibilities before they are fully prepared. Their impatience tells them to "get on with it," but if they listen carefully, they may hear God telling them to prepare well so that they can present themselves as workmen who do not need to be ashamed and who correctly handle the word of truth. (2 Tim. 2:5)

Many young women do not fully perceive marriage to be a responsible job. It requires skill and expertise in many areas, especially in the art of homemaking. Preparation is a vital matter. Jonathon Swift said, "The reason why so few marriages are happy is because young ladies spend their time in making nets, not in making cages."[5]

We can learn a lesson from the Chinese Bamboo

tree which is watered and cared for five years, and then in a six-week period grows nine feet all at once. If the proper time is taken to develop the character, skills and maturity necessary for strong marriages, they are more likely to flourish.

Jesus spent many years preparing for a ministry in which he was only engaged two to three years. The success of that ministry, however, was so great it has made an impact on the world for almost 20 centuries.

Preparation is essential if we are to be successful in our work. Let's not rush the harvest.

Accepting God's Will

Discerning God's will for my work may be difficult, but it is even more difficult to accept his plan singlemindedly once I have discerned it. Today we find it hard to accept the responsibility of aged parents. There seems to be no fitting time to give to this good work. Careers interfere, or children interfere, and this responsibility is rejected. God, however, knew the blessings it would bring to both the aged and the young, and so his plan included a provision for the care of parents by children, just as it did for the care of children by parents. There is a mutual blessing in this provision. When this work is presented to me I must accept it singlemindedly as God's chosen work for me at that time.

Singlemindedness implies a narrow focus which is not popular in today's world in which versatility is in vogue. Being able to do a variety of things is important to many of us. This lesson was impressed on me one lovely spring day when I was riding with a friend admiring the beautiful spring flowers in our town. I commented on the pleasure I get from flowers. As we rounded the corner of my yard she laughingly said, "Oh, yeah. You really like flowers, don't you? Where are yours?"

As she drove away I took a look at my yard and felt very poor indeed. It was true. My yard was no beauty spot. I stood looking at its well-worn ball diamond in the back yard, the old rubber tire sandbox, the odd assortment of flowering bushes, including lilacs from my mother's farm, an unnamed wild bush planted by our nature loving daughter, and a gigantic sprawling oak we refused to have trimmed because our son could reach the lowest limb and pull himself up with pride. While I was appraising my deficiency in spring beauty a carpool van drove up and our five children came popping out from all directions calling, "Mother, we're home." My heart overflowed with pride, and I was reminded that I was not in the flower growing business. I was in the child growing business, and what a beautiful, flourishing business it was!

It is difficult to keep a single-minded attitude, to be content doing the business appropriate for today, and that only. We feel compelled to branch out, to dabble in everything, ashamed to admit that we have limitations. The truly single-minded attitude of Mary who was not troubled about many things, but had only one focus, frees us from the guilt of saying "no" to good, but untimely, tasks. Young mothers must be aware that the job at hand is a demanding and important one, and that "no" can be the wisest word in their vocabulary.

Dependency on God Essential

Not only must my work be God chosen, but my work efforts must be coupled with an awareness of my dependency on God. The most unlikely prospects were chosen by God to accomplish important tasks. Humility characterizes each of them. They perceived their inability and God's ability to accomplish their tasks. Sarah, who was ninety years old and could see only humor in bearing a child, was appointed by God to be the mother of Israel (Gen. 18:10-19). The Syrian maid, a youth on foreign field who was performing menial tasks, served as God's mouthpiece to save the Aramean ruler, Naaman, from death by leprosy (2Kings 5:10). God used Gideon, identified by himself as least in his own family and of the weakest clan in Manasseh, to strike down the Midianites (Judg. 6:15). Rahab, a Gentile with a tainted reputation, was listed on the honor roll of the faithful for helping the Israelites destroy Jericho (Heb. 11:31). God chose Mary, a young, poor virgin, a very unlikely prospect for a job of importance, to become mother of the Messiah (Matt. 1:18-23).

What did these hand-picked vessels of God have in common? They were all in situations of helplessness and each was willing to be used by God in whatever way he chose. They conceded to God with such remarks as, "I am the Lord's servant. May it be to me as you have said" (Luke 1:38). Rahab, not feeling worthy to claim God as her Lord, said, "For the Lord your God, He is God in heaven above and on earth beneath" (Josh. 2:1). Each saw God as the potter and self as the clay.

The recognition that the success or failure of my work efforts is determined by God, the initiator of my work, should free me from the stress of the quest for success. It should enable me to work more, not less, diligently since my motivation is intrinsic, not extrinsic. Being able to see a result or a reward in sight is not what motivates me, for I am working as "unto the Lord."

Under this system a woman will devote her whole hearted effort to her marriage whether she is married to a loving, devoted husband, or to a critical, difficult one. Her task master is Christ and her efforts to please are directed toward him. She is not an eyepleaser. Her work does not vary depending on the earthly situation.

Our Works Must Glorify God

Most importantly, my work must be of such a nature as to glorify God, not self. Jesus told us: "Let you light so shine before men that they may see your good works and glorify your Father in heaven" (Matt.. 5:16).

This mindset implies a "John the Baptist" attitude, who admittedly was not that light, but merely a reflector of that light. John saw the necessity of moving away from the forefront of importance to allow God's light to shine.

If the impact of my work effort only reflects as far as my light allows, then it is insignificant indeed. However, if it reflects God's light, its distance has no limit, for his light gives light to every man that comes into the world.

Getting out of the way and letting God's glory take precedence is not always easy. Even Moses, a great man of faith, craved a little recognition for his work and heaped glory on himself by saying, "Must we bring water for you out of this rock?"(Num. 20:10) Just as the glory stopped short of the father, Moses' leadership stopped short of the promised land.

The only possibility for my works making an eternal difference is for them to reflect the glory of God. I, within myself, am nothing. Yet, God can take my efforts and multiply them a thousand fold.

Quality Work

In order to glorify God with my work, quality labor is imperative. Let's look at some of the descriptors of quality work that are mentioned.

1. Willingness

There is little commendation due a wife and mother who serves her family, meeting their every need, if her attitude is one of imposition. God loves a cheerful giver, and so do family members. A baby learns at an early age whether he or she is a delight to the mother, or an infringement on her activities. It gives a child inner security to know that care is provided willingly.

Teaching Bible classes, visiting the sick, taking in food when it is needed can all be viewed as opportunities rather than chores. A happy mindset lets the light of God shine through. "The light of the eyes rejoices the heart, and good news refreshes the bones." (Prov. 15:30)RSV.

Perhaps the reason God didn't delegate exact amounts of time or money to be given is because some possess greater potential in the area of generosity than do others. A small task performed willingly is preferable to "surrendering my body to the flames"[6] out of compulsion.

This is the same principle found in Proverbs concerning mindset.
"Better is a dinner of herbs where love is than a fatted calf with hatred" (Prov. 15:17). "Better is little with the fear of the Lord than great treasure with trouble" (Prov. 15:16).

It was this willing mindset that caused the Jews to

91

rebuild the walls of Jerusalem in spite of persecution and ridicule. Nehemiah accredited it to the fact that the people "worked with all their heart" (Neh. 4:6).

When we are working with our heart we don't count time, we simply enjoy it. Jacob volunteered to work for seven years for Laban in exchange for his beautiful daughter, Rachel. But the years seemed like only a few days because of his love for her. This was truly a labor of love (Gen. 29:20).

Isn't this true for all of us? When our work is motivated by love no chore is too difficult. What mother adds up hours she has spent nursing a sick child? She is working whole heartedly and voluntarily, so time is irrelevant compared to accomplishment.

The elderly and disabled view work with fondness. They long for days of accomplishment when energy was plentiful and their labor was needed. When they do have opportunity to be productive, they show more appreciation for this opportunity than do younger people who take their work opportunities for granted.

My ninety year old daddy spent several days in the hospital receiving cancer treatments. When he was released the doctor told him he could do whatever he felt like doing. When we drove up to his farm he didn't go inside, but headed straight to the garden where he began his battle against the weeds. When he came in to eat he was quoting the last verse of the **Village Blacksmith**.

Toiling, rejoicing, sorrowing,
Onward through life he goes;
Each morning sees some task begin,
Each evening sees its close;
Something attempted, something done,
Has earned a night's repose.[7]

He was happy to be able to accomplish, even in a small way, a useful task. Work was created for pleasure and should be viewed accordingly. "Whatever your hand finds to do, do it with all your might" (Eccles. 9:10).

2. Diligence

God extols the industry of the ant in Proverbs 6:6 and uses her as an example to us. We may compare ourselves to the worker ant, which does the majority of the work in the community, plus caring for the young and building the nest. She constructs her nest intricately, building chambers and galleries, sometimes excavating under logs or stones or in decayed trees. She works diligently at the job asigned her.

Likewise, the virtuous woman of Proverbs 31 was diligent in her work, working willingly with her hands, refusing to eat the bread of idleness. No work was beneath her dignity. She was not selective in her chores, but stooped to the most menial task, whether working in the fields planting the vineyard, gathering in food from great distances, or sewing garments for her family. Solomon said, "The desires of the diligent are fully satisfied" (Prov. 13:4).

3. Persistence

Willingness and diligence are not enough. We must also work persistently. My mother had a saying which reminded us of the importance of finishing the job at hand.

When a task is once begun
Never leave it till its done
Be the labor great or small
Do it well or not at all.

Paul said it differently. "And let us not grow weary while doing good, for in due season we shall reap if we do not lose heart" (Gal. 6:9).

We cannot afford to quit when we get so near the finish line. Work opportunities are always available, but they are subject to change. As we grow older we often feel less productive, but we are seldom so void of opportunity and energy that we can't, in some way, be a blessing to others. Exhortation, admonitions, and prayer are always needed. These may seem trivial, as accomplishment goes, but seizing the opportunity at hand is never trivial in God's sight.

Conclusion

Paul is an example to us of one who had the right work ethic. He worked willingly, diligently, and persistently through hardships and persecutions. He never gave up. In his letter to Timothy near the end of his life he was able to say confidently, "I have fought the good fight, I have finished the race, I have kept the faith. Finally there is laid up for me the crown of righteousness, which the Lord, the righteous Judge, will give to me on that Day, and not to me only, but also to all who loved His appearing" (2 Tim. 4:7-8).

If we are not longing for his appearing it may be that we are not persisting in our work and therefore are not in need of rest. We, like Paul, want to be able to say with confidence, "I have fought, I have finished, I have kept." There is no quitting time.

The book of Revelation gives us a glimpse of the triumph of those who persevered through trials and hardships to the end. It is a reminder to us to keep on keeping on. "Be faithful, unto death, and I will give you the crown of life" (Rev. 2:10).

1. 2 Thessalonians 3:10.
2. 1 Timothy 5:3.
3. James 1:22.
4. Luke 12:20.
5. Glenn Van Ekeren, *Speaker's Sourcebook* (Englewood Cliffs, New Jersey: Prentice Hall, 1988) Used by permission.
6. 1 Corinthians 13:3.
7. Henry Wadsworth Longfellow, "Village Blacksmith,"*Best Loved Poems To Read Again and Again* (New York, New York: Galahad Books, 1979), p.53.

THOUGHTS FOR DISCUSSION

I. Discuss changes which have taken place in the woman's work world during the last few decades and how they have affected her choices for work.

2. Why is it difficult for women to attain a proper balance between work and rest?

3. We often experience feelings of guilt over the good deeds left undone. What teachings of God can help us maintain peace in spite of limitations?

4. What attitudes toward work do we want to instill in our children, and how do we accomplish this? Does undue emphasis on recreation affect work attitudes?

5. Paul warns of the danger of wives trying to please their husbands rather than God. Is this a current problem, and if so what can we do to change our view? Read and discuss Paul's teaching on this in 1 Cor. 7:34.

Prayer Thought: "Help us to view work as an opportunity and a blessing. Forgive us when we complain."

COMFORTING

Chapter Eight

GOD, OUR COMFORTER

The Lord is near to those who have a
broken heart, and saves such as have a
contrite spirit. (Psa. 34:18)

God is our comforter. This quality of God, perhaps
more than any other, draws him from the realm of
perfection into our realm of imperfection, from his all-
sufficiency to our realm of need. It brings him into the
here and now world and involves him in our daily
struggles. If we picture God as the creator who sits on
his throne, removed from our mortal realm, then we do
not know God, the comforter, and we may feel deserted
in our time of sorrow.

Why Does God Allow Suffering?
A misconception of God causes some to turn
from him rather than *toward* him in their time of grief.
They perceive the unchanged situation to be the sign of

an uncaring, uninvolved God. Questions arise in their minds. Why does God allow pain when he is able to stop it? Isn't comforting unnecessary since the pain itself could be alleviated? Could we not compare him to a doctor who would treat a cancer patient with pain medicine when he knew and had access to the cure?

Parents who have faced crises with their children know better. They have the power to stop the immediate pain, but because of the broader view they realize the significance of enduring the present suffering to avoid a much worse fate.

These words may sound familiar: "I don't want to go to school today. My stomach hurts when I do arithmetic and the teacher makes me do it anyway." He is pushed gently out the door. "It'll be all right. You'll catch on to arithmetic and pretty soon your stomach won't hurt anymore."

Or, "Mommy, please, don't make me get a shot. Please." "Yes, Dear, we don't want you to take measles. Measles will hurt a lot worse than a shot."

The eighteen year old decides that college is too far away and homesickness is too painful. "I'm coming home and work a couple of years first. Then I"ll go to college later." "Why prolong the misery?" you ask. "Now is as good time as later."

"Marriage is not what it's cut out to be. You just don't know him, Mama. Sometimes he's obnoxious. I'm thinking of coming home." "No, Dear. We're all obnoxious sometimes. That's why it's for better or worse. Hang tough."

We know that our parents allowed us to suffer hardship when it was for our good, and we thank them for it. Why can't we trust God to allow only those trials that will work for our good? Instead, we become

Marthas, criticizing God in our hearts, saying, "Lord, if you had been here, my brother would not have died."[1] We must recognize that God's presence does not stop pain or death. He was there when his own son died. He was grieving. He was hurting, but he was certainly there. We can rejoice in his sorrow for it was that same sorrow that gave birth to our comfort.

If we can rejoice in God's sorrow why can't we rejoice in our own suffering?

In this you greatly rejoice, though now for a little while, if need be, you have been grieved by various kinds of trials that the genuineness of your faith, being much more precious than gold that perishes, though it is tested by fire, may be found to praise, honor, and glory at the revelation of Jesus Christ. (1Pet. 1:6-7)

Does God allow us to be afflicted with pain and then console us in our suffering?

Does a loving parent chastise his son, yet grieve with his son over the pain? Undoubtedly. What mother, when probing with a needle in search of a thorn, does not groan inwardly with her child? Parents inflict pain because of their love. God does the same, and he groans inwardly because of our pain.

God's Provisions for Our Comfort

God knew that with mankind would come sin, and with sin would come grief and pain. While we were still in the mind of God, he devised a plan for our comfort. God could not dwell in the presence of sin, but he would not leave us comfortless. Provisions were made for peace in the midst of a sinful world.

1. Prophets

First, God raised up prophets who were to be his instruments of direction and instruction. A message from God is one source of comfort. David recognized that comfort is found in God's "rod and staff." There is security in guidance and direction. Left without instruction from God, man would be like sheep without a shepherd.

Secondly, and equally important, the mission of the prophets was to console the people when they had gone astray. "Comfort, yes, comfort my people," says your God. "Speak comfort to Jerusalem" (Isa. 40:1).

The prophets' messages of comfort were not delivered through words alone; their lives symbolized their message. Jeremiah's life was stripped bare of popularity and success. He was forbidden by God to marry, and so experienced loneliness. He was the bearer of a message of doom, so he experienced rejection. He was thrown into a pit, driven from his homeland and went through life weeping, yet, he was not forsaken by God. He was given frequent reminders of his commission to become a prophet. Jeremiah accepted God's comfort and became his fearless servant.

Ezekiel lost his beloved wife, but he was not allowed to mourn openly for her just as Israel was not to mourn for Jerusalem. Ezekiel, instead consoled Israel with words of hope and revival and plans for a glorious future. Ezekiel's personal grief enabled him to impart God's consolation to Israel more effectively.

The word Nahum means "comfort." Nahum's name and mission were the same. He was to comfort Judah through the fall of Ninevah.

Hosea was told to take a wife, an unfaithful wife,

whom he would love, forgive, and reinstate after losing her to a sordid life of adultery. He could then speak to Israel out of real life experience concerning God's forgiveness, love, reinstatement and consolation.

2. A Savior

While these great men of God could proclaim a message of comfort which included God's forgiveness and reinstatement of Israel, their real consolation lay in the prediction of a Savior, one who would embody God's power, and would not only promise forgiveness, but would forgive. He would remove guilt. He would remove remorse. He would change the unchangeable. This was the message of hope and comfort offered to the Israelites, and it is our message of comfort today. They knew him only in promise. We know him by his life, a most remarkable life. Jesus, God's own son made mortal, entered a sin filled world, reaped the unjust consequences of our sin and became a "man of sorrow, acquainted with grief."[2]

Why? So that he could comfort us as one friend comforts another. When he gives the loving invitation, "Come unto Me, all you who labor and are heavy laden and I will give you rest" (Matt. 11:28), we know that he is speaking as one familiar with burden bearing. He can empathize with our plight and extend God's comfort as only one sufferer can do to another.

Therefore, in all things He had to be made like His brethren, that He might become a merciful and faithful High Priest in things pertaining to God, to make propitiation for the sins of the people. For in that He Himself has suffered, being tempted, He is able to aid those who are tempted. (Heb.2:17-18)

What could I suffer that he has not already suffered? He groaned in pain. He sweat as though it were blood. He knew the grief of rejection. He knew the grief of desertion. He experienced humiliation. He knew the pain of loneliness, of life without a mate, a child, or a home. He even experienced the separation from God inevitable in the presence of sin - our sins - as he hung on the cross.

Familiar with pain, Jesus had an intense desire to comfort other sufferers. The host of a wedding feast near the brink of social calamity had a problem that Jesus could not overlook. His compassion, even in a small matter, was so great as to cause him to work an untimely miracle. The grief of two sisters in the death of their brother caused Jesus to weep, even though he knew it was only a temporary situation (John 11:4-5, 35). A sinking Peter who envisioned himself with the faith of Jesus but who had, in reality, faith the size of a mustard seed, was sustained by the hand of Jesus. A gentle, loving rebuke helped Peter to accept himself as a weak human being, not a divine champion (Matt. 14:28-31).

Distress in any fashion captured Jesus' attention. A hungry multitude, a wayward woman, a pack of lepers, a blind man, and disciples troubled by his departure all received comfort appropriate for their plight.

Jesus has the background to empathize with problems, the longing and desire to comfort, and the power to sustain in any situation. That power is equally available to us today. So why do we carry around burdens as those who have no God? Our lives should be characterized by peace and tranquility, but instead they are filled with guilt, disappointment, insecurity, inadequacy, and hopelessness.

> Said the Robin to the Sparrow
> I should really like to know
> Why these anxious human beings
> Rush around and worry so.

> Said the Sparrow to the Robin
> Friend, I think that it must be
> That they have no Heavenly Father
> Such as cares for you and me.[3]

We simply are not tapping into God's resources. We are like the man who lived in poverty all his life not knowing there was oil just under the surface of his land.

Zones of Discomfort

We have many zones of discomfort, but provisions were made by Christ for comfort in each area. First, there is the area of insufficiency. There are important jobs to be done and strength insufficient for the tasks. There are children to be reared, deadlines to meet, classes to teach, ministries to accomplish, hospitality to extend, and we lack wisdom and know-how to get it all done.

Failure to tap into his power reminds me of a poem.

> Worry is an old man with bended head
> Carrying a load of feathers which he thinks
> are lead.[4]

God, who is All-Sufficient, offers the solution.

> If any of you lacks wisdom, let him ask of God, who gives to all liberally without reproach, and it will be given to him.

(James1:5)

Be anxious for nothing, but in everything,
by prayer and supplication, with
thanksgiving, let your requests be made
known to God: and the peace of God,
which surpasses all understanding, will
guard your hearts and minds through
Christ Jesus.. (Phil. 4:6)

In light of God's promise there is no excuse for insufficiency.

Insecurity in our salvation is another area of discomfort. Like David, our sins are ever before us. We are so aware of our weaknesses and failures that we lose sight of the Author and Perfector of our faith.

My sheep hear My voice and I know them
and they follow Me: And I give them eternal
life; and they shall never perish, neither
shall any one snatch them out of My hand.
My father, who has given them to Me, is
greater than all; and no one is able to
snatch them out of my Father's hand.
(John 10:27)

It is God's stability, not our own, that offers security to the believer. We realize, like Paul, that nothing good lives in us, but that God can rescue us from our sinful condition. His forgiveness and reconciliation become our comfort.

When our imperfections bring about hopelessness or despair, his words usher in hope:

I am the resurrection and the life; He who
believes in Me, though he may die, he
shall live, and whoever lives and believes
in Me shall never die. (John 11:25-26)

Let not your hearts be troubled; you believe in God, believe also in me. (John 14:1)

Another zone of sorrow is loneliness. We have all been overwhelmed with void or emptiness at times in life. Old age is known to be a time when losses, change, and adjustments occur leaving unimaginable void. The familiar disappears. Old age is not, however, the only lonely time in life. Working with college students I am made aware of the adjustments that occur when young men and women leave home for the first time, branch out into the unknown, form new attachments which are not always easy, and make decisions which will affect their entire lives. Without a personal relationship with God a sickening loneliness sets in, making life almost unbearable. Studies show that suicide is prevalent among college students, becoming the second most common cause of death.

God's Holy Spirit

Jesus does not forsake us in our loneliness. When he returned to Heaven he did not leave us void of himself, but gave us the Holy Spirit to dwell within us. This is one of the richest blessings we acquire by being his children. To the apostles Jesus said:

And I will pray the Father, and He will give you another Helper, that He may abide with you forever, even the Spirit of truth, whom the world cannot receive, because it neither sees Him nor knows Him, but you know Him, for He dwells with you and will be in you. I will not leave you orphans; I will come to you. (John 14:16-17)

Conclusion

God is <u>with</u> us and <u>in</u> us, but we sometimes forget that he is also <u>for</u> us. "If God is for us, who can be against us?" (Rom. 8:31).

His Spirit bears witness with our spirit that we are his children. We can never be alone with a Father who is omnipresent. There is no way we can escape him even if we tried. What greater comfort could there be than having the constant presence of God?

Peace I leave with you; My peace I give
you; not as the world gives do I give to you.
Let not your heart   be troubled, neither let
it be afraid. (John 14:27)

1. John 11:21
2. Isaiah 53:3
3. Charles L. Allen, *God's Psychiatry* (Old Tappan, New Jersey: Fleming Revell Co., 1985), p.94.
4. Glenn Van Ekeren, *Speaker's Sourcebook* (Englewood Cliffs, New Jersey: Prentice Hall, 1988), p.388. Used by permission.

THOUGHTS FOR CONSIDERATION

I. Do some of our blessings come in the guise of evil? If so, who sends them?

2. Why is it easier to accredit God with our blessings that come in desirable packages than with the blessings of hardship that help refine our faith?

3. Some people are drawn closer to God through trials while others go far from him. Discuss factors which influence these reactions.

4 Discuss the comfort of touch as found in Jesus' treatment of the following:

> Deaf man (Mark7:31-37).
> Leper (Matt. 8:2, Mark 1:40).
> Peter (Matt. 14:28).
> Blind Man (Mark 8:23).

5. Discuss the similarities in the lives of the prophets and Jesus. How did their backgrounds equip them for ministering to the discomforted?

6. We are reminded by the Holy Spirit that we are God's children. (Rom. 8:16) How does this reminder take place?

Prayer Thought: "We know, O Lord, that you are close to the broken hearted, and that you hear the cries of the distressed. Comfort them with your love and tenderness.

Chapter Nine

COMFORTED TO COMFORT

Blessed be to the God and Father of our Lord Jesus Christ, the Father of mercies and God of all comfort, who comforts us in all our tribulations, that we may be able to comfort those who are in any trouble with the comfort with which we ourselves are comforted by God. (2 Cor. 1:3-5)

God has given women a special ability in the area of comfort. He compared his comfort to Israel to a mother's comfort of her child. "As one whom his mother comforts so I will comfort you; and you shall be comforted in Jerusalem" (Isa. 66:13). "That you may feed and be satisfied with the consolation of her bosom" (Isa. 66:11).

The thought of a mother's comfort has been the inspiration for many songs. The mention of a mother's embrace, her lullaby, and her nurturing trigger pleasant memories in most of us.

God instilled in mothers, even within the animal world, the desire to comfort and protect their own. Jesus uses this parallel to convey his love to the Jews.

O Jerusalem, Jerusalem, the one who kills the prophets, and stones those who are sent toher! How often I wanted to gather your children together, as a hen gathers her chickens under her wings, but you were not willing! (Matt. 23:37)

If an animal comforts by instinct, how much more do we, as mothers, thrive on being able to soothe and comfort our children?

Our oldest daughter, married but still childless, was living six hundred miles away from us when she had a third miscarriage. Her voice was shaky as she called on the phone to tell us what was happening, and I knew the grief and disappointment she was bearing. No duties were too pressing, no plane ticket too expensive to prevent my going to her. Reaching her bedside and gathering her into my arms I asked how she felt. She said, "Fine, now that you are here." That was all my motherly heart wanted, to know there was comfort in my presence.

While we feel so adept at soothing the hurt of our own family members we often feel inadequate in reaching out to those we know less well. We may conclude that comforting is not our gift. However, the admonitions to bear one another's burdens (Gal. 6:2), and to weep with those who weep (Rom. 12:15), are given to all. Would God expect us to comfort, but not equip us with the tools essential to accomplish the task?

Burden bearing can be accomplished through many means. Like so many tasks God leaves the "how" up to us. We need to inventory our gifts and find a way that is natural and comfortable to us.

Comfort in Touch

The physical message of touch is an important one. Jesus touched the lepers, the blind man, and the little children. He demonstrated the power to soothe through the human touch.

My friend lay dying of cancer. Her pain was intense. I sat in the hospital room wishing for a way to comfort her, but in the presence of pain I found myself tense and mute. A young mother, Debbie Ganus, who was also her friend, entered the room, heard the sobs, and went straight to her bed. She gathered her into her arms and stroked her hair back from her face. Her words were gentle. "I wish I could take your pain away, or at least bear some of it for you. You are being so brave." The sobs subsided. The tension relaxed. This young lady continued stroking her forehead and rocking her gently in her arms. She had a special knack for comfort. I observed her and marveled at her shamelessness in touch and words.

Words Offer Comfort

There is comfort in words, but words may not flow easily for some. Afraid of saying the wrong thing we say nothing at all. Silence can convey apathy. Any message is preferable. Though we flounder around and express our concern poorly, others will be able to sift through our message and receive it as it was meant.

One lady told me that when her husband was unjustly dismissed from his job many came to express their regrets, but she couldn't help taking note of those who didn't say anything. She interpreted their silence as consent. She knew that all of those people who were quiet did not agree with the supervisor, but she had no way of knowing unless they expressed their disagreement.

Another lady, whose husband divorced her for another woman, moved from her hometown because so few people expressed their support. She interpreted their lack of communication as condonement of her husband's actions. Our lack of message communicates a negative one in many instances.

A Written Message

If we are not gifted in the spoken word a written message will suffice. My mother has a writing fluency which she has used to bless many people. Her opportunities for outreach would have been limited except for her pen. She writes notes of encouragement to those who have a lapse in zeal. She expresses her sympathy and concern for the grieved. When people have to move outside the community she corresponds with them to keep them informed and to help them make the transition well. Her daily letters were a great comfort to me when I was a homesick college freshman. I suppose the greatest comfort she has offered has been to the hundreds of Africans who knew nothing of Christ and with whom she corresponded and administered the World Bible School lessons. She brought many from a world of darkness into a world of light through her pen.

Listening

If words are difficult for us perhaps we can offer a sympathetic ear. There is an art to listening. Many troubled people need a sounding board. They are not seeking counsel or sympathy. They merely need to talk, and in recounting their stories they resolve the conflict, themselves.

Erma Bombeck impresses us with the need for

being good listeners in the following personal story:

There were thirty whole beautiful minutes before my plane took off...time for me to be alone with my own thoughts, to open a book and let my mind wander. A voice next to me belonging to an elderly woman said, "I'll bet it's cold in Chicago."

Stone-faced, I answered, "It's likely."

"I haven't been to Chicago in nearly three years," she persisted. "My son lives there."

"That's nice," I said, my eyes intent on the printed page of the book.

"My husband's body is on this plane. We've been married for fifty-three years. I don't drive, you know, and when he died a nun drove me from the hospital. We aren't even Catholic. The funeral director let me come to the airport with him."

I don't think I have ever detested myself more than I did at that moment. Another human being was screaming to be heard and in desperation had turned to a cold stranger who was more interested in a novel than the real-life drama at her elbow.

All she needed was a listener... no advice, wisdom, experience, money, assistance, expertise or even compassion... but just a minute or two to listen.[1]

James reminds us to be quick to listen, and slow to speak.[2] We can hardly go wrong to sit quietly and devote our full attention to another person's story.

Ministering to Needs

Physical deeds and gifts seem to be of little importance at times of grief, and yet, they are necessary. Food must be provided. Its nourishment even soothes and comforts to some extent. When my uncle died people sent in more food than could be eaten. My aunt decided to quit accepting the excess food, but her sister advised her not to. "Keep the pies and freeze them. They represent your friends' love and that is the only way they know to show it." She took this advice, accepted all food as a message of love and preserved it for future needs.

There are many acts of helpfulness to be done if we are looking for them. One man I knew went to a home in time of a tragedy and sat for hours reading funny books to the four year old. This kept his mind occupied and off the troubles at hand. It was a simple task but it helped this child cope with sadness.

Music Offers Comfort

In considering avenues of comfort let's not forget music. Music was invented by God as a universal language of consolation. It relieves stress. It soothes frayed nerves, and dissolves tension. It inspires and lifts us above this world's cares. What mother has not enjoyed the effects of a lullaby on her disgruntled baby? It gives her a feeling of sufficiency to hear the cries subside and feel the body relax from hearing the familiar melody of her voice.

David used the gift of music to soothe the king. The harp which had provided inspiration for him (1Sam. 16:23). The years spent in developing the skill of harp playing were aptly put to royal use.

One of the beauties of group worship is the power

of comfort as well as exhortation that comes through song. The multiple voices, united as one, lift us above the temporal and give us a glimpse of the eternal. God specifically designated variety in singing, psalms, hymns and spiritual songs, each working its purpose on the divergent needs of the people (Col. 3:16).

We make distinctions in sacred and secular music, but there is much of the sacred in the secular. What could be more soothing to the spirit than Beethoven's Moonlight Sonata, or who could leave a concert having heard one of Mozart's Concertos without having a more positive outlook on life?

Depression is very prevalent in today's world. We see its symptoms exhibited in sadness, anxiety, insomnia, withdrawal and the inability to function normally in routine affairs. Whether physically, spiritually, or emotionally induced, it is very real. We may not be qualified to counsel the severely depressed (a professional may be needed), but we can show our love and concern. Giving a gift of music may provide the solace they crave. A tape or record which has uplifted us may be more expedient than offering a personal gift of music for which we have little or no talent, and which might seem artificial or inappropriate.

Attitude Toward the Discomforted

One of our greatest means of providing comfort (or discomfort) is the attitude we show. The grief brought on by mistakes and sin is often the most painful kind. The mistake can't be corrected. Its damage is done. But the remorse is keen.

"If only I hadn't let her date so young."

"Why didn't we have family devotionals?"

"If I had been more aware of his needs maybe he

wouldn't have turned to someone else."

"My parents always had time for me. How did I let myself get too busy for them?"

"Why did I become so intimate with him?"

When we are full of remorse we need soothing, not scolding. Who needs Job's friends to visit, point the finger of guilt, and shake the head in disdain? Job ably described his friends when he said, "Miserable comforters are you all!" (Job 16:2)

We must remember the advice of Jesus. "Let him who is without sin cast the first stone" (John 8:3). Surely we have all experienced the remorse of sin. Its guilt is painful but its memory can help us to empathize and say, "But for the grace of God, there go I."

Charity

There is so much good in the worst of us,
And so much bad in the best of us,
That it ill behooves any of us
To find fault with the rest of us.[3]

We learn from Job what would be welcome in times of pain and grief. He told his friends that if they were in his condition his mouth would encourage them, and comfort from his lips would bring them relief.[4] A young lady who suffered great disappointment from being childless told me that the one thing no one ever said to her in the way of encouragement was, "God loves you." She said that would have offered her the greatest comfort of all.

God's word is full of encouragement and positive edification. If we have it hidden in our hearts we can offer scripture as comfort. What could be more positive than these words:

Therefore you now have sorrow; but I will see you again and your heart will rejoice, and your joy no one will take from you. (John 16:22)

Let not your heart be troubled; you believe in God, believe also in Me. (John 14:1l)

There is therefore now no condemnation to those who are in Christ Jesus, who do not walk according to the flesh, but according to the Spirit. (Rom. 8:1)

For I consider that the sufferings of this present time are not worthy to be compared with the glory which shall be revealed in us. (Rom. 8:18)

Accepting God's Comfort

Even more important than our attitude may be our example. How can we extend God's comfort if we are discomforted?

When Paul compared these present sufferings with future glory he spoke as one familiar with suffering. He was a survivor. He was triumphant. He was not overcome by the world, nor was he down-trodden. After describing his trials in 2 Corinthians 11:23-26 he concludes with this response: "I delight in weaknesses, in insults, in hardships, in persecutions, in difficulties. For when I am weak, then I am strong." Paul was a mentor of comfort. He had learned to live comfortably under all circumstances and so is able to coach us in that direction.

Personally, I was slow in learning that accepting God's comfort is a prerequisite to offering it to others. A baffling situation arose in our home when our second

116

daughter, Cheryl, began having grand mal seizures. Brain tests confirmed our fears. She had epilepsy. She was put on medication for three to five years, or until the brain wave patterns were normal. "Don't worry," we were told. "80% are controlled with medicine, and she may outgrow it. In the meantime she should avoid heights, swimming and driving. Otherwise, treat her normally. A healthy home atmosphere is important."

How could I treat her normally when I didn't feel normal myself? Every nerve in my body was frayed. A pain shot up my hip when I moved, and I couldn't walk without a limp.

Initially Cheryl had a healthy attitude toward her illness. She discussed it openly with her friends. The few restrictions placed on her were accepted without complaint, even though swimming was her favorite sport.

Unfortunately she was one of the 20% not controlled with medicine. Another seizure occurred, then another, and another. I became so rattled that I slept lightly at night. One cough, or one child's trip to the bathroom brought me quickly to my feet. My body stayed alert for emergency action. I looked and felt tired. Eventually I went for a checkup. "You're in good health," I was told, "just a little tense."

That was an understatement. I constantly relived the nightmare of the seizures. I watched Cheryl's every move, and kept my ears alert to trouble. A hair brush dropping on the floor was all it took to send me into a state of panic. If she showered too long I threw open the door to check on her. (Two seizures had occurred in the tub.)

So much time and attention were concentrated on Cheryl that our other children showed signs of discouragement. They longed for the happy, carefree atmosphere our home had known.

Cheryl's attitude began to change also. She became sensitive to remarks of friends, resentful of my protectiveness, and restrictions. I tried to console her by telling her that God never allows hardships to befall us which are greater than we can bear, that he helps us bear our burdens. But she remained disquieted.

One day after praying for wisdom to impart the peace of God to my family I searched the scriptures for help. When I read 2 Corinthians 1:3-5 I knew God was answering my prayer. He was speaking directly to me through this passage.

Blessed be the God and Father of our Lord Jesus Christ, the Father of mercies and God of all comfort, who comforts us in all our tribulation, that we may be able to comfort those who are in any trouble with the comfort with which we ourselves are comforted by God.

How could I extend the comfort of God to Cheryl when I, myself, was discomforted? God was saying to me, "The problem is yours. My comfort can best be shown through you. But you must first receive it." I had not accepted God's comfort because I had not fully accepted his will.

At this point my prayer changed from a plea for Cheryl's good health and peace of mind to a plea for my relinquishment. "She is yours, Lord," I prayed. "You can heal her. You can help her bear her infirmity, or you can take her to be with you. You are her creator, and I know that you love her even more than I."

Having emptied myself of worry and tension I was filled with the comfort of God. Relief swept over me. The problem was no longer mine, and neither was the solution. It was in God's hands.

At that point our home's atmosphere began to change. Anxiety was replaced with tranquility. Tensions relaxed and peace was restored. Cheryl blossomed. She again became God's triumphant child.

The external situation didn't improve for a long time. Not only did Cheryl's seizures continue but different forms of the same illness showed up in two more of our children. There were severe headaches, petit mal seizures, and black-out spells. I came to realize through all of this, that my confidence cannot hinge on external circumstances, but on God who controls them.

Today good physical health as well as mental health blesses our family, for which we are grateful. Cheryl is a happily married mother of three beautiful, healthy children, and is enjoying a seizure free life. With those struggles, however, came the realization that inner peace is a gift from God that can prevail through any crisis, and that we can comfort others only to the extent that we, ourselves, accept the comfort of God.

Conclusion

David said, "For You will light my lamp; The Lord my God will enlighten my darkness" (Psa.18:28). Jesus said, "You are the light of the world" (Matt. 5:14). I am continually being illumined by God. If I move away from him my light grows dim. If I move toward him my light fans into flame. My primary responsibility then, is to stay near the source of light so that I can illumine the path for others, comforting them with the comfort I received from God

1. Erma Bombeck, *if life is a bowl of cherries-what am i doing in the pits?* (New York, New York: Random House, Inc., 1978), pp. 248, 249.
2. James 1:19
3. Author Unknown, "Charity," *Best Loved Poems To Read Again and Again* (New York, New York: Galahad Books, 1986) p.74.
4. Job 16:5..

THOUGHTS FOR DISCUSSION

l. The dictionary defines comfort as aid, encouragement, relief from distress. Discuss some personal methods of encouraging the discouraged and relieving distress.

2. Invite a physician to discuss depression and other forms of mental illness with the class, perhaps making suggestions for support we can offer.

3. Can you think of a time in life when it was difficult for you to accept God's comfort? Discuss the circumstances which sustained you.

4. Jesus speaks to us saying, "It is I. Be not afraid." What circumstances obscure our vision of Him?

5. How significant is the comfort we offer others if we have not introduced them to God, the greatest comforter of all? Substantiate your answer.

Prayer Thought: "May we accept your comfort which is always available so that we may, in turn, be able to comfort those around us."

PRAYING

Chapter Ten

LORD, TEACH US TO PRAY

Prayer is beautifully described by Dwight Bradley in his writing entitled What is Worship?
It is the soul searching for its counterpart.
It is the thirsty land crying out for rain.
It is a candle in the act of being kindled.
It is a drop in quest of the ocean.
It is a man listening through a tornado for the Still Small Voice.
It is a voice in the night calling for help.
It is a sheep lost in the wilderness pleading for rescue by the Good Shepherd.
It is the same sheep nestling in the arms of the rescuer.
It is the Prodigal Son running to his Father.
It is a soul standing in awe before the mystery of the Universe.
It is a hungry heart seeking for love.
It is a heart of love consecrating herself to

her lover.
It is Time flowing into Eternity.
It is my little self engulfed in the Universal Self.

It is a man climbing the altar stairs to God.[1]

Opportunity of Prayer

It is a great privilege to be able to approach the creator of the universe directly through prayer. We, of all God's creation, are the only ones granted an open line of communication. The birds of the air and the lilies of the field enjoy God's abundant care, but they have no way of responding to him. Continual access to the mind of God is one prime evidence of his love. Jesus, while removed temporarily from the source of glory, stayed in constant touch with that glory through prayer. He recognized prayer to be a great privilege, and so he prayed because he *wanted* to pray. He wanted to communicate with his Father. Communicating with one we love is always pleasant. We don't have to engage in a notable conversation, nor have a particular reason to converse to enjoy the day to day chit chat and the bonding that takes place as a result.

Constancy of Prayer

Prayer was a part of Jesus' daily routine. He spent hours in the garden alone with God. On every occasion and in all circumstances he prayed. He prayed for the needs of others: their physical infirmities, their sins, sanctification, faithfulness, forgiveness, their being filled with the Holy Spirit, and their salvation (John 17:9-26). He prayed for his enemies, even those who crucified him (Luke 23:34). He prayed for himself: for glorification, for deliverance from the cross and from temptation (Matt. 26:39, 42). He prayed for little children (Matt. 19:13-15). In preparation for his ministry, he spent forty days in the wilderness in fasting and prayer (Matt. 4:1-2).

Luke tells us, "Jesus went out *as usual* to the Mount of Olives, and his disciples followed him" (Luke 22:39). This shows the constancy of prayer in his life. He knew, just as we know today, that deficient communication breaks ties and dulls the emotional bonding. This is true in marriages. Counselors stress the importance of steady communication. Some sort of regular, planned exchange of thoughts must take place, or else, when they are together there is little to say because contact has been lost. Jesus knew this to be our nature and so he made prayer a regular part of his life as an example for us.

Scriptures emphasize the importance of making prayer a routine part of our lives.

Praying always with all prayer and supplication in the Spirit... (Eph. 6:18)

Rejoicing in hope, patient in tribulation, continuing stedfast in prayer. (Rom. 12:12)

Pray without ceasing. (1 Thes. 5:17)

But in everything, by prayer and supplication, with thanksgiving, let your requests be made known to God. (Phil. 4:6)

Blessings of Prayer

Prayer changes things. We can observe the differences in praying and non-praying people.

Consider the difference in Jesus and his disciples. There is a noted contrast in their strength to overcome temptation. While Jesus prayed the disciples slept (Matt. 26:37-46). When trials came Peter denied the Lord, the others deserted their hero and fled, while Jesus remained strong, surrendered, and serene (Matt. 26:68-75). The strength administered by an angel made the difference. Jesus wanted that strength, and so he prayed.

Prayer is a great defense, but it is also a good offense. We don't need to wait until we reach the end of our own resources to pray. How much more fitting to turn to him at the beginning of battle! Jesus' battle against Satan was won in the desert. He spent 40 days preparing for battle, and when Satan confronted him with temptations he was able to withstand because he had conceded to God at the onset (Matt. 4:1-11).

Again, Jesus prepared for struggles with Satan in the Garden of Gethsemane. Through prayer which was so intense as to cause him to sweat as though it were blood, Jesus won his battle before it began (Luke 22:43-44).

Paul describes the Christian warfare in Eph. 6:10-18, showing the battle to be a spiritual one and our armor to be spiritual in nature. After having armed ourselves completely with belt, breastplate, shoes, shield, helmet and sword, we are to take the offensive position in battle and pray. *Pray?* Are we not to attack? We have prepared for battle and prayer implies the battle is not ours but God's. This is true. Our part is to concede to God through prayer. It is our best, and sometimes our only, offense. God can and will fight our battles for us just as he did for Christ. This is one of the greatest blessings of prayer.

Mentor of Prayer

Knowing that we should pray, and developing the desire to pray does not necessarily ensure our ability to pray. Even the disciples who walked with God through the footprints of Jesus felt deficient in ability to communicate with him through prayer. Whether it was humility they developed by recognizing the gap between the minds of God and man, or a desire for increased effectiveness in their prayer lives, they entreated, "Lord, teach us to pray" (Luke 11:1).

Jesus did not insist that they had a natural talent for praying nor censure them for asking, but merely honored their request. This prayer of example is found in Matthew 6:9-13 KJV.

Recognition of the Father

Our father which art in heaven, Hallowed be thy name.

Jesus begins his prayer with a statement of *recognition..* It is important to know the one we are addressing. Approaching God as *Our Father* indicates that we are aware of him as our source. We recognize our earthly father to be the donor of life on earth and our Heavenly Father to be the donor of all life, including eternal.

As a father he also becomes our provider. Even an earthly father wants to give us the things we need to make life good and to bless us, whether they be trials or triumphs. Even more so our *Heavenly Father* who has all wisdom to know what we need and complete access to supply those needs provides for us in an ample way.

The relationship of *father* indicates the closest of kin, a loving, benevolent and merciful parent to whom we dare reveal our innermost confidences. When we know him as a *Father in Heaven* we couple that tenderness and concern with power and sufficiency.

Isaiah observed the superiority of God's dwelling place to ours and compared this to the inner being as well. "As the heavens are higher than the earth so are my ways than your ways and my thoughts than your thoughts"(Isa. 55:9). This gives us confidence to pray. We observe God's ability and our inability, his wisdom and our lack of the same. We, like Isaiah, upon seeing God, see ourselves and recognize our state of need. "Woe is me, for I am undone"(Isa. 6:5). Recognizing my undone state I will be in a frame of mind to pray, and my immediate response is to glorify God.

Hallowed be thy name. A name is a symbol, important only because of whom it identifies. We are to revere the name of God because of the Being of reverence it represents. God, in setting Jesus above all others, .."gave him a name that is above every name, that at the name of Jesus every knee should bow, in heaven and on earth and under the earth" (Phil. 2:11). "Jesus" was a common name at the time he was born. It was not the out-of-the-ordinary name that made it special, but the out-of-the-ordinary Being which that name represented which set that name above all names. We can understand the importance of first recognizing God, and giving glory to him before petitioning or entreating him in behalf of self or others.

Relinquishment
Thy kingdom come. Thy will be done on earth as it is in heaven.

A most comforting thought is that God who made

us, who knows, and who cares, triumphs. We want God's will to be done. Let's thank God for over-ruling and for triumphing in our lives. If we knew our will would prevail we would be insecure, like spoiled children who are used to having their own way, unhappy in their willfulness. Praise God I have been relieved of the pressure of being number one in my own life. I am not the master of my fate nor the captain of my soul, but I have been bought with a price (1 Cor. 6:19-20). As his child I joyfully concede to him.

In the course of my life I have prayed a few willful prayers, bent on having my way regardless of God's will. Some of those prayers have been answered affirmatively, but have never proven to be a blessing. As I have matured in faith I realize that I want God's will to prevail.

The most comforting message I received when my daddy died was from a cousin who wrote, "And so again his kingdom comes, his will is done, and another great saint is added to that cloud of witnesses." Accepting the will of God is easy when we are aware of the great love he has for each of us.

There has been an ongoing debate as to whether hardships, deaths, and seeming calamities can be God's will in the lives of his children. In my opinion, which is an imperfect opinion, everything which happens in the lives of God's children, except sin, is God's will. That is my security. I can accept hardships and trials and even calamity if I realize that they have passed through God's sifter and been deemed suitable for me, not more than I can bear. This, therefore, becomes God's will for me.

Request
Give us this day our daily bread.
This is the prayer of *request*. Why ask when our Father knows what we need even before we ask? Isn't it his part to make the decision and ours to accept?

There is a plaque which reads, "God gives the best to those who leave the choice to him." Our daughter, Laurie, has this attitude toward prayer. She is diligent in praying, but compliant enough to prefer that God make the choices in her life. She has complete confidence in his ability to choose. Yet, most of us are more opinionated, and want to have a voice in outcomes. God endowed us with discerning minds, minds which have preferences, wants, wishes and longings, and I believe he expects us to express them.

Speaking from a parent's perspective, the child who never makes his wishes known is not the easiest to satisfy. He may drift along, seemingly happy while the parents remain unaware of his unmet needs. Then, as an adult he lets it be known that he felt some resentment of his position in the family, or of the treatment he received. He harbored unmet longings which he had never made known.

One of our daughters told us after she was married that she never got to have company when growing up like her sisters did. I was under the impression that everyone had company: over-night guests, weekend guests, parties, after school dates, evening dates, unexpected guests. But, in the hurry scurry of life I had overlooked one seemingly content daughter who never asked for much nor made known any deficiencies in her home life.

God taught us to ask, and to keep on asking. Even though he knows our needs he wants us to communicate them to him. "By prayer and supplication, with thanksgiving, let your requests be made known to God" (Phil. 4:6).

We often are inhibited about praying over the details of our lives. We feel that the God of the universe who is involved in matters of such magnitude as life and death could not possibly be interested in our minute petitions. Everything in our lives, however, is small compared to God's greatness. As children's prayer requests sound trivial to us, "Please, help my dog to get well," or "Help it not to rain my ball game out," our prayers also involve matters which are small in God's eyes. He created us with minute minds, yet promises to hear our petitions.

It is interesting to note that God, while Lord of the universe, is also a God of detail. The intricate instructions he gave in building the tabernacle impress us with this. A curtain was to be made of blue, purple and scarlet yarn and finely twisted linen, with cherubim worked into it by a skilled craftsman. The work of an embroiderer was required to make the curtain for the entrance of the tent, and we who have worked in embroidery know how tedious it can be to make even one small flower. God has never shunned detail. He gave instructions for making the lamp stand of pure gold with flowerlike cups shaped like almond flowers with buds and blossoms to decorate it. Think of the hours of skilled labor it took for these men to fashion the lamp stands according to God's directions.

How can we surmise that God, who is involved in such intricate detail, does not care about the small things in our lives? If it is big enough to concern us, it concerns him.

Renewal

Forgive us our debts as we forgive our debtors.

There is *renewal* in prayer. What joy compares to that of a clear conscience? Through prayer we are forgiven and cleansed, but Jesus makes that forgiveness contingent on our willingness to forgive. We may wonder why. A forgiven state is a sinless state. Where bitterness and resentment abide, the ugliness of sin is still present. If we have a small capacity for forgiving, we also have a small capacity for accepting God's forgiveness.

> Do not judge, and you will not be judged. Do not condemn, and you will not be condemned. Forgive, and you will be forgiven. Give and it will be given to you. A good measure, pressed down, shaken together and running over will be poured into your lap. For with the measure you use, it will be measured to you. (Luke 6:37)

Monte Cox, an African missionary, told a story about buying corn in Africa when he was working there. The amount of corn you might get for $2.00 depended on the attitude of the seller, though the price per unit was the same. One woman would sell a bucket with several empty cobs in the bottom and a level measure across the top scarcely filling the container. Another would pour in corn, shake it down, reach in with her arm and stir it to take out air pockets, heap it until it formed a pyramid at the top and began to run over. Then she would say, "Here is your $2.00 worth of corn." However, he said they both realized he was given more than his money's worth. This was good measure, pressed down, shaken together and running over. He was fortunate to find a seller of generous mindset.

We are fortunate to have a judge of generous mindset. Jesus heaped on forgiveness. He forgave the woman caught in adultery and instigated forgiveness from her peers. He even forgave those who didn't ask for, nor want forgiveness, as he died on the cross.

Peter asked for a limit to be set on the amount of forgiveness expected of us, but Jesus removed the boundaries, saying even seventy times seven.[2] In our littleness we would like to think we can reach a saturation point in forgiving others, but when we consider the amount of forgiveness we want from God, we want no restrictions placed. We have all been forgiven much, and so we should be willing to forgive in the same proportion.

My grandmother's merciful judgment of others impressed me. When she heard of a wrongdoing she immediately said, "Well, he (or she) had a good heart, though." She assumed a good intent. When she heard of an atrocious act committed she presumed mental illness. We laughed at the extreme measures she took to give benefit of the doubt, but we were so thankful for her benevolence when it came to our mistakes. We could tell all and know she would be merciful in her judgment. And we all want bountiful mercy in judgment, heaped up, pressed down, and running over. This type of judgment is an indicator of love, and forgiveness is an outgrowth of love.

As we love we forgive, and as we forgive we are forgiven. Let's be generous in our love and forgiveness, using the bountiful measure that we want measured to us.

Realization

Lead us not into temptation but deliver us from evil . For thine is the kingdom and the power and the glory forever.

The realization that I am human, therefore weak, compels me to ask for deliverance from sin. The prayer that was commended by Jesus was that of a man who merely acknowledged his inability and God's ability: "Have mercy on me, a sinner" (Luke 18:13).

Paul reiterated the same thoughts in Romans 7:18-20, 24-25.

"For I know that in me (that is, in my flesh) nothing good dwells; for to will is present with me, but how to perform what is good I do not find. For the good that I will to do , I do not do; but the evil I will not to do, that I practice. Now if I do what I will not to do, it is no longer I who do it, but sin that dwells in me...Who will deliver me from this body of death? I thank God - through Jesus Christ our Lord!"

There is an adage that states: "The Lord helps those who help themselves." We are relieved, however, to know that the Lord also helps us when we cannot help ourselves. We are weak and easily tempted. When tempted, we are often overcome because we rely on ourselves. When we are overcome we become discouraged and resolve to do better, but we are drawn away again by temptation and again we sin. Paul tells us the only hope we have is found in Christ's power, because we are powerless.

Youth, in its blaze of passion and vigor, offers limitless temptations which are stronger than our human nature can withstand. The power that comes through prayer needs to be instilled early in life before those days come when peer pressure exerts so much force.

Romantic relationships pull at the heart and involve all of the human emotions and if there is conflict between the head and the heart it is almost impossible to triumph without God's help. A girl falls in love with a boy whom she realizes will never be the godly leader in the home. She lacks courage to lay aside the relationship and faith to envision life without him. Where does she get her strength? Only from God who is able to deliver. She believes in chastity. He insists on intimacies she conscientiously opposes. How does she maintain her self-respect? Through prayer.

The only way we can overcome the evil one is through God. John tells us in 1John 4:4, "You are of God, little children, and have overcome them, because He who is in you is greater than he who is in the world." Our access to the greater one is through prayer.

Conclusion

Jesus was constantly in touch with the Father through prayer. He prayed when alone and when he was with others. He prayed in all circumstances, becoming our mentor in prayer. The realization that God possesses the kingdom, power, and glory made prayer the most significant resource in his life.

1. Andy T. Ritchie Jr., *Thou Shalt Worship The Lord Thy God* (Austin, Texas: Firm Foundation Pub. House, 1969), pp. 4, 5. Used by permission.
2. Matthew 18:21-22

THOUGHTS FOR DISCUSSION

I. Have you ever prayed a willful prayer and had it answered? Discuss its outcome.
2. Give other reasons for praying besides those discussed in this chapter.
3. Do we need to teach our children to pray or do they pray spontaneously as they know God?
4. Is it easy to pray for forgiveness in the same degree that we forgive, or would we be more comfortable if our forgiveness were not contingent on our willingness to forgive?.
5. What are some ways we can hallow God's name?
6. What are the purposes and blessings of group prayer? Find and discuss examples of it in the New Testament.

Prayer Thought: "We know, Oh Lord, that our longings lie open before you, and that you know our needs before we ask. We want to thank you for teaching us the importance of asking anyway."

Chapter Eleven

OUR PRAYERS ARE ANSWERED

We want to be like Jesus, and so we pray. There are some people, however, who believe in prayer as a necessary form of communication and as a fulfillment of Jesus' teaching, but they expect it to initiate no change. Jesus' prayers resulted in change. If our prayer lives are fashioned after his, they will also result in change.

There are so many misunderstandings related to prayer that the **Huck Finn** mindset is not uncommon.

Miss Watson she took me in the closet and prayed, but nothing come of it. She told me to pray every day, and whatever I asked for I would get it. But it warn't so. I tried it. Once I got a fish-line, but no hooks. It warn't any good to me without hooks. I tried for the hooks three or four times, but somehow I couldn't make it work. By and by, one day, I asked Miss Watson to try for me, but she said I was a fool. She never told me why, and I couldn't make it out no way. I set down one time back in the woods, and had a long think about it. I says to myself, if a body can get anything they pray for, why don't Deacon Winn get back the money he lost on pork? Why can't the widow get back her silver snuffbox that was stole? Why can't Miss Watson fat up? No, says I to myself, there ain't nothing in it.[1]

A very godly man was being honored on his 100th birthday. A few statements were read about his life showing that he had committed the New Testament to memory in early life and that he had made prayer a daily part of his routine. When asked if he could cite some answers to his prayers he looked puzzled, then thoughtful, then said, "No, I don't know of any answers I've received."

I feel sure there were many answers to those prayers, but he was not expecting them to initiate a response. For the next few weeks I pondered this and tried to recount the answers I had received to prayers. It was not as easy as I had anticipated. I knew there were countless times that I had remarked certain events were answers to prayer, but I had to delve into my memory to recall them.

Could it be that we pray, our prayer is answered, and we straightway dismiss it from mind? Having received what we requested, we turn to other pursuits without dwelling on thanksgiving and praise for the answer we received. Perhaps we even take credit for the change ourselves, and fail to acknowledge God as the source of change. Personal testimony to others about how God has answered our prayers helps cement these answers in our minds as well as theirs. The Israelites had periodic feast days to remember God's attentiveness to their cries for help when they were in Egyptian bondage (Ex. 12:15-20). These special occasions kept God's direct involvement in their lives in the forefront of their minds.

James indicates that our prayers have the same response from God as those of great men in the Bible.

> Elijah was a man with a nature like ours,
> and he prayed earnestly that it would not
> rain and it did not rain on the land for three
> years and six months. And he prayed
> again, and the heaven gave rain, and the
> earth produced its fruit. (James 5:17-18)

Our prayers, then, can be just as powerful and effective as Elijah's, causing a change in the circumstances around us. God is as accessible to me as he was to Aaron when he entered the tabernacle or to Jesus when he was on earth. The veil is rent! God hears and answers today just as he did then. His answers may take a different form from what we expect, but we can be assured of an answer.

Direct Answers

Let's look at some prayers which were answered *directly*. These are what we usually speak of when we say God answers prayers. A request is made. God grants the request giving an affirmative answer immediately. We have many examples of direct answers in the Bible.

Hannah poured out her soul to the Lord, praying out of great anguish and grief because of her barren state.

> So it came to pass in the process of time,
> Hannah conceived and bore a son, and
> called his name Samuel, saying,
> 'Because I have asked for him from the

Lord.' (1 Sam. 1:20)

Eliezer, servant to Abraham, was sent to get a wife for Isaac. He realized the significance of the decision and he entreated God for help. "Now let it be that the young woman to whom I say, 'Please let down your pitcher that I may drink,' and she says 'Drink and I will also give your camels a drink'- let her be the one whom you have appointed for your servant Isaac...Before he had finished speaking, behold, Rebekah came out with her pitcher on her shoulder" (Gen. 24:14-15). This was an immediate, affirmative answer.

We could also mention Gideon's prayer for the sign of dew on the fleece (Judg. 6:36-40), Hezekiah's prayer for longer life (Isa. 38:1-8), and Samson's prayer for strength to pull down the temple posts (Judg. 16:28-30). There are many others also which make us aware that God heard and answered prayers in Bible times.

Were direct answers given only then or can we expect them today as well? Remember, Elijah was cited as a man *just like us.* A story was told me by a friend, **Jerry Hill**, who lives in New York City. He said that he and a friend decided to take their boys for an outing in the woods to let them explore and learn about God's creation through nature. After a few pleasant hours they gathered for prayer and his friend prayed in this manner: "Lord, this is such a good experience and we want our boys to know all about your creation so, please, send a hummingbird for them to watch and learn about its ways." At this point Jerry said that he became very uncomfortable. He thought, "Couldn't he have asked for a bird without being so specific? What will it do to our sons' faith if God doesn't send a hummingbird?" They unpacked lunch and sat down to eat it when, sure enough, there came the hummingbird they had prayed for. It hovered nearby and they watched it for about fifteen minutes before it left. Jerry marveled at the man's faith in asking. The hummingbird was a good gift, and was not to be consumed on self, so why not ask?

Stipulations of prayer

There are some stipulations regarding our requests. First, they should be unselfish in nature. We might ask, "Is this something which will help me to be what God created me to be? Is it in keeping with his purpose for me?" We sometimes might justify our selfish requests saying we will use what we are given to bless others or to bring glory to God. **Milton** refuted these false pretenses by observing in his sonnet, <u>On Blindness</u>, that God has thousands at his post to do his bidding and to accomplish his purposes. He does not need our accomplishments or gifts.

The movie, **Amadeus,** portrays a man who aspired to the gift of genius in music that Mozart was given. He prayed for the gift to bring glory to God. It was given, rather, to one inferior to himself, without his noble aspirations. Because he felt the gift was misgiven he became embittered, turning against God and man.

Whether truth or fiction, this story could be written about many of us. We pray for a gift under the pretense of wanting to glorify God, when in reality, if we are truly selfless in our aspirations, we will be willing to let God be God. We will let him give his gifts at will, and we will seek wisdom to recognize and use what he gives us.

The second stipulation in asking is that we ask in faith. We can learn lessons in trust from little children. They pray specific prayers, pertinent to their immediate needs and they expect an answer. If we are aware of their prayers we will see that God attends to their petitions and answers their requests affirmatively on many occasions.

When our daughter had five small children, including two-year-old twin boys who carried every object straight to the commode, she paid a plumber twice in one month to unstop it. The third time he was called he could see an expandable toilet tissue holder which had gone in closed and then expanded so it couldn't come out. He worked two hours before declaring it an impossibility and suggesting they buy a new commode. Finances were tight and she was on the verge of tears when her five year old daughter, Mollee, said, "Mommy, we don't have to worry; we can just pray." This they did and on the next try the plumber retrieved the stuck object. Mollee was not surprised, just relieved they had remembered to pray.

We can learn a lot about prayer from children. Their trust is abundant and faith unlimited. Perhaps this is one of those instances when we need to become as little children to enter the kingdom of heaven.

A lady in our community had the faith to make a prayer request of her small study group. She asked them to pray that she give birth to a baby. She had two adopted children who were adored but she also wanted one by natural birth. The following month she conceived. That child is her Samuel, figuratively speaking, *asked of God.* (1Sam. 1:20)

We have varying degrees of faith and we can only ask accordingly. I have two aunts who each have strong faith in God's ability and willingness to answer prayer, but they have very different attitudes about what we should pray for. Aunt Ebby prays for every little thing that affects her life, while Aunt Hilda believes the small things can run their course. Aunt Ebby was suffering from heart failure and then took cold and congestion also. She sent for Aunt Hilda to come for a visit. When Aunt Hilda arrived she found her much stronger than she had expected and inquired about her improvement. "Oh, the ladies in my prayer group prayed for my cold and I'm over it," she said. "Well, while they were praying why didn't you ask them to pray for your heart too?" Aunt Hilda asked skeptically. "Oh, Hilda, I didn't have *that* much faith," she responded. Isn't it true that we can only expect answers in proportion to our degree of faith in asking? (James 1:6)

Our Response to Direct Answers

When God answers our prayers directly what is our response? Do we sometimes accredit the changed circumstance to fate? My daddy told a story of a man who called on God for help as he fell from a tall tree but immediately retracted his prayer saying, "Never mind, Lord, I've caught on this limb." We are like that at times. We focus on the changed circumstance, but not on the changer. On the other hand, we may fall into step with the nine infamous lepers who took Jesus' gift for granted and simply failed to say, "thank you" (Luke 17:11-17). Hopefully, we will capture the spirit of David who accredited God with his help and healing and poured out thanksgiving from his heart for God's attentiveness to his prayers (Psa. 40:1-5).

Disguised Answers

It may be easy to accredit God with affirmative, direct answers, but God doesn't always answer directly. Sometimes his answers are disguised.

We prayed for my oldest daughter and her

142

husband to be given a baby. She had a record of miscarriages and we knew God could preserve her pregnancy, but instead he gave her a precious, bi-racial child by adoption. This was an answered prayer, but the answer was not what we expected.

I like the following poem:

God's Strange Answers
He was a Christian and he prayed.

He asked for strength that he might do greater things; but he was given infirmity that he might do better things.

He asked for riches that he might be happy; he was given poverty that he might be wise.

He asked for power that he might have the praise of other men; he was given weakness that he might feel the need of God.

He asked for all things that he might enjoy life; he was given life that he might enjoy all things.

He had received nothing that he asked for; all that he hoped for.

His prayer is answered. He is most blessed.[2]

Jesus' mission on earth was often obscured to his followers. He came to bring comfort, but he brought trials to accomplish this. " These things I have spoken unto you, that in Me you may have peace. In the world you will have tribulation" (John 16:33). He came to give life, but he asked that we lay our lives down. "He who finds his life will lose it, and he who loses his life for My sake will find it" (Matt. 10:39).

Even though he was known as the Prince of Peace, he acclaims that he did not come to bring peace, but a sword (Matt. 10:34). There is conflict between good and evil, light and darkness. His mission is often obscured; therefore, it is not strange that his answers to our prayers are often not as they seem. Not having the mind of God, we cannot begin to fathom his plan for our lives nor the reason for the strange answers to our prayers.

These disguised answers are hard to discern unless we are looking intently and with expectation. When my uncle, who was a Christian, was very sick with cancer his daughters prayed fervently that he be healed. As he lay in the casket they were encompassed with peace and faith because they said their prayers were answered. Pain was gone. Peace was restored to him, and he was indeed healed.

Delayed Answers

There are times when God's answers to our prayers are *delayed*. We are impatient and decide that God isn't listening. We must remember that God is not bound to our time frame. "But do not forget this one thing, dear friends: With the Lord a day is like a thousand years, and a thousand years are like a day" (2 Pet. 3:8).

David reminds us to "Wait for the Lord; be strong and take heart and wait for the Lord" (Psa. 27:14). David battled with his enemies many years before being delivered. He knew the importance of waiting.

God heard the Israelites when they cried out because of their bondage. He sent Moses to rescue them from slavery, but before they were rescued, their circumstances grew worse. Their work was increased, their materials decreased, and their production was expected to be maintained. Even Moses said, "You have not rescued your people at all" (Ex. 5:23).

God did, however, rescue them. Some of the Israelites may have died in the meantime, many had become discouraged, and I'm sure all had begun to question whether God really heard their cries. But, from the written account, we realize that the prayers of the Israelites were heard and their plea for help was answered in God's time frame, not man's.

Gratification is sometimes sweeter when delayed. The joy of Christmas to a child is in part the anticipation of good things to come. They have experienced good gifts at this season before, and they have faith they will receive again. Their hope and happiness mount with time. An engagement period before marriage makes the anticipation grow. There is time for planning, for hoping and dreaming. Love is embellished.

The Israelites might not have had the courage to leave their homes in Egypt and launch out to the unknown if God had delivered them from bondage immediately. Their strength and desire for delivery grew with time.

Because God does not initiate an instant change does not mean there will be no change. Abraham and Sarah must have grown weary with waiting. They had been promised a son. They expected to receive a son. Even after waiting until he was a hundred years old Abraham believed God (James 2:23). It was this persistent belief that secured his spot on the honor roll of the faithful (Heb. 11:7-10, 13).

God promises to hear our prayers. How much do we believe in him? A special blessing is promised those who wait on the Lord. "They that wait for Jehovah shall renew their strength; they shall mount up with wings as eagles; they shall run, and not be weary; they shall walk, and not faint" (Isa. 40:31).

That passage was set to music, and I like the conclusion of the song that says, "Teach me, Lord, teach me, Lord, to wait." Patience does not come easily for most of us. We want what we want, and we want it now. An increased confidence in God's ability to answer and in his promise to hear can sustain us through some dark hours of waiting.

Negative Answers

Waiting, however, does not always ensure a positive answer to prayer. God does not paint a one sided picture of prayer by telling us only about the affirmative answers, but he gives examples of the hard, negative answers as well. *Denial* is one way God answers prayer.

David prayed for his child to live. He fasted, wept and continued in prayer, but God denied his request. The child died (2 Sam. 12:16-18). Paul begged God to take away the thorn in the flesh. Three times he entreated, but the request was denied (2 Cor. 12:7-9). He was given what he needed, but not what he wanted. Even Jesus, God's only son, asked for release of pain in that terrible death on the cross, but his request, too, was denied.

If God denied the requests of men of faith like David, Paul and Jesus, who are we to raise our voice against him for denying us? What parent continually and consistently grants his child's every plea? A wise parent sees the broader picture and can look into results that might take place. God has seen our lives laid out before him like an open book which he can read from cover to cover. With our limited view how can we discredit prayer, saying God does not hear just because he overrules our decisions?

I knew a man who lost his son in World War II. He said, "There's nothing to prayer. I prayed every day for my son to return safely, but he died." Receiving a negative answer was the same as receiving no answer at all to him.

Attitude Toward Negative Answers

No matter how much insight we have into God's answers we will always find denial hard to accept. We can be thankful for that great cloud of witnesses who have set an example before us of acceptance. Job endured many hardships with the grit and determination expressed in his statement, "Though he slay me, yet will I hope in him"(Job 13:15). So did Habakkuk. He affirmed his trust in God's presence regardless of how harshly God dealt with him.

> Though the fig tree may not blossom, nor fruit be on the vines; Though the labor of the olive may fail, And the fields yield no food, though the flock be cut off from the fold, and there be no herd in the stalls, yet I will rejoice in the Lord, I will joy in the God of my salvation. (Hab. 3:18)

Contrast the attitudes of King Ahab and King David when denied an important wish. King Ahab turned his face to the wall and sulked because Naboth refused to sell him a vineyard. His attitude said, "If my request is not granted I'll bask in my misery." On the other hand when King David lost the child he had prayed for so diligently , he got up, washed and ate saying,

While the child was still alive, I fasted and wept; for I said, 'Who can tell whether the Lord will be gracious to me, that the child may live? But now he is dead; why should I fast? Can I bring him back again? I shall go to him, but he shall not return to me.
(2 Sam.12:22)

Acceptance of hard answers is not easy. It takes unconditional trust in God's love for us and in his wisdom to make the best decisions. It is my aspiration to be able to pray wholeheartedly the following prayer of **Horatius Bonar**.

> Thy way, not mine O Lord,
> However dark it be!
> Lead me by thine own hand,
> Choose out thy path for me.
>
> Smooth let it be or rough
> It will be still the best.
> Winding or straight, it leads
> Right onward to thy rest!
>
> I dare not choose my lot;
> I would not if I might.
> Choose thou for me, my God,
> So shall I walk aright.
>
> The kingdom that I seek,
> Is thine; So let the way
> That leads to it be thine
> Else I must surely stray
>
> Take thou my cup and it
> with joy or sorrow fill

As best to thee may seem;
Choose thou my good or ill.

Choose thou for me my friends,
My sickness or my health;
Choose thou my cares for me
My poverty or wealth.

Not mine, not mine the choice
In things great or small;
Be thou my guide, my strength
My wisdom and my all.

Conclusion
I want to imitate my Lord in every aspect of his life so that I may acquire his virtues. I want his strength to overcome the evil one. I want his wisdom, and his discernment. I want his ability to concede to God unconditionally. The only path to these virtues is through a regular and active prayer life, one fashioned after his example of complete trust in God to hear and answer prayer.

1. Mark Twain, *Huck Finn* (New York, New York: Penguin Books Ltd.,l959), p.20.
2. Andy T. Ritchie J., *Thou Shalt Worship The Lord Thy God* (Austin, Texas: Firm Foundation Pub. House, l969), p.102.

THOUGHTS FOR DISCUSSION

I. There is a country song, "Thank God for Unanswered Prayers." Recite some negative answers you have received for which you are thankful.

2. Why is wisdom promised unreservedly? (Jas.1:5) Discuss the faith required to act on our best judgment after having prayed for wisdom.

3. "Ask and it shall be given you," is told us by Jesus. Yet, we have all had requests (seemingly good requests) turned down. How can this be explained?

4. Discuss disguised answers to prayer. How do we know the difference in God's disguised answers and in nature taking its course?

Prayer Thought: "We believe you hear and answer our prayers, but help our unbelief!"

FRIENDSHIP

Chapter Twelve

GOD, OUR FRIEND

What a special blessing God bestowed on us when he chose to become our friend! He could have revealed himself to us as a dictator, a guardian, or a puppeteer, but he chose, rather, one of the most precious relationships on earth, that of friendship. He knew that we could not be left to walk alone on this earth and so he offered himself - his thoughts, his Spirit, his companionship, his very presence - to free us from loneliness and to support us in our daily walk with him.

Sharing of Intimacies

True friendship doesn't just happen. Planting the seed is not enough, it must be cultivated and nurtured. God made friendship a priority. He practiced the give and take that is so essential to friendship. The intimacy of thoughts he exchanges with us is one of the greatest signets of his friendship. Although his thoughts are higher and nobler than ours (Isa. 55:8-9), he has chosen to disclose them to us because he is our friend. He has disclosed his grief and disappointment over sin, his remorse over having created mankind, and his hopes and plans for a shared eternity (Mark 3:5, Matt. 23:37, Gen. 6:5-8, John 14:1-4). He made us his confidants. What an expression of friendship! There is no greater intimacy, even in marriage, than the unveiling of the heart. While our tendency is to guard our thoughts tenaciously, it is impelling to friendship that we reveal as well as listen. This requires vulnerability, laying ourselves bare before each other, exposing our inner beings. A counselor may lend a listening ear, but this hardly constitutes friendship. There must be reciprocation.

In observing God's relationship to Moses we see an intimate exchange of thoughts. " So the Lord spoke to Moses face to face as a man speaks to his friend" (Ex. 33:11).

While God was giving the law to Moses on Mt. Sinai, the Israelites turned away to serve their own creation, a golden calf. God talked to Moses about his anger and his desire to destroy his people, and then he listened while Moses reasoned with him and presented his viewpoint.

Why should the Egyptians speak and say,
'He brought them out to harm them, to kill
them in the mountains, and to consume
them from the face of the earth'? Turn from
Your fierce wrath, and relent from this harm
to Your people.So the Lord relented from
the harm which He said He would do to His
people.. (Ex. 32:12)

There was mutual exchange of ideas, and receptiveness to each other's point of view. God was influenced by man. He, the omniscient one, was influenced by the unknowing. Why? Because of the bond of friendship.

152

Again, we see God revealing his thoughts to Abraham as he disclosed his plan to destroy Sodom. "Shall I hide from Abraham what I am doing?" (Gen.18:17) He then confessed his anger and disappointment toward his people and his plan to wipe them from the face of the earth.

Abraham responded by saying,

Would You also destroy the righteous with the wicked? Far be it from You to do such a thing as this to slay the righteous with the wicked, so that the righteous should be as the wicked; Far be it from you! Shall not the judge of all the earth do right? (Gen. 18: 24, 25)

The Lord was receptive to Abraham's plea, amended his plan, and saved the few righteous souls in that city. The counsel of a friend was accepted by an all-wise God.

Jesus exemplified this quality of intimate exchange by confiding in his apostles. He discussed his upcoming death and departure, his plans to prepare a new earth, his hopes for their steadfastness and their re-uniting with him. He then concluded with a statement of intimacy.

No longer do I call you servants, for a servant does not know what his master is doing; but I have called you friends, for all things that I have heard from My Father I have made known to you. (John 15:15)

He not only shared his intimate thoughts with friends, but also his most personal and momentous occasions. Peter, James and John were taken to the mountain of transfiguration where they witnessed his awesome change and triumph over all other lawgivers. Peter exclaimed wholeheartedly, "Lord, it is good for us to be here" (Matt.17:4).

We all like to be privileged to the inside scoop. The more personal experiences and feelings that are shared, the greater the bond of friendship. In fact, our tapestry of friendship is woven of those special moments in life shared with those we love most. Who can replace the friend who stood beside you on your wedding day, or the one who experienced with you the joy and apprehension of high school graduation? And what about the college roommate who was there when you first caught a glimpse of what God wanted you to do with your life, and when you first fell in love; or the friend who was there when your babies were born, or when a loved one died? Jesus left a legacy of friendship by involving others in his special moments.

Exchanges of small intimacies are important too. A seemingly small one Jesus shared was that of foot washing. Peter, afraid of this degree of familiarity, refused the washing, but Jesus pointed out the necessity of intimacy on the earthly level in order to achieve intimacy on the eternal level. Peter, then wishing for all the privileges of friendship replied, "Lord, not my feet only but also my hands and my head "(John 13:9).

Most of us find it easier to share our good times than our bad times. We miss some good opportunities for friendship by pretending we have no troubles. Our human nature wants us to appear unperturbed and in control. Jesus solicited friendship in his hour of need. When he was suffering agony over his upcoming crucifixion, he took his closest friends to the garden to pray. There was no facade, no pretense of toughness or self-sufficiency. He bared his heart before them, acknowledging his agony and dread of the upcoming events, and begging his father to remove them, if he so willed. The strength gained from this hour of prayer sustained Jesus through the strenuous hours ahead, and though his friends missed the significance of the occasion by sleeping, they may have recalled this hour many times in later life when they faced trials of their own.

Accepting Graciously

Valuable also to friendship is the ability to accept graciously. While Jesus was privileged to full access, he demonstrated the ability to receive from his friends. Mary annointed him with perfume valued at the price of a year's wages, a lavish gift indeed! (John 12:3-5) We might think of it as a wasteful, useless, short-lived gift, but Jesus esteemed it as priceless, a gift of love.

He entered Jerusalem in a flourish of praise and accepted it with dignity, even while knowing this praise would shortly turn to vindictive cries for his death.

Jesus accepted hospitality. He had no home to offer in return. He provided no food but the bread of life. Yet, he welcomed the opportunity to go to Bethany and enjoy the warmth of his friends' home.

There is a plaque which reads, "Friends ask of each other." Jesus not only accepted but he asked. At the time of his death he solicited care for his mother from a friend. John must have felt very special to be asked a personal favor, because he immediately took Mary into his own home. Could this be why he referred to himself as the apostle whom Jesus loved?

It endears a friend to me to be asked a favor. I was delighted to have a friend call and ask to use my house for her surplus guests one weekend when we were going out of town. This same friend asked me to come to her home and sit with her sick daddy one day when she needed to be away. I felt so special to be entrusted with this job, and the bond of friendship was stronger because she deemed me a close enough friend to ask of me.

Trust

Friendship also involves trust. God testifies to our friendship by entrusting us with a part of his very own being. "The Spirit who dwells in us yearns jealously" (James 4:5). He placed his Holy Spirit inside us to strengthen us and to identify us as his. We were cautioned not to "quench" the Spirit and not to sin against it because it is God in us. What greater gift could he have entrusted us with than a part of himself?

He also entrusted us with his gospel. Who but God's friends could he trust to be sole messengers of the good news of salvation for which Jesus died? This was an awesome responsibility. Even in these days of supersophisticated communication systems, the story of salvation, the greatest story ever told, rests entirely on the shoulders of God's friends. There is no alternative plan. Does it not seem strange that God could deem us responsible enough and trustworthy enough to convey his love message to the entire world? (Matt. 28:28-30, Mark 16:15-16)

Trust, in friendship, must be twofold. God, himself, is trustworthy. He cannot lie.

Paul, a servant of God and an apostle of Jesus Christ, according to the faith of God's elect and the acknowledgement of the truth which is according to godliness, in hope of eternal life which God, who cannot lie, promised before time began, but has in due time manifested His word through preaching, which was committed to me according to the commandment of God our Savior...(Tit. 1:1-3)

Thus God determining to show more abundantly to the heirs of promise the immutability of His counsel, confirmed it by an oath, that by two immutable things, in which it is impossible for God to lie, we might have strong consolation, who have fled for refuge to lay hold of the hope set before us. (Heb. 6:17-19)

The assurance of God's honesty is the anchor for our friendship. Without belief in his promises there would be no friendship. Abraham was called a friend of God (James 2:23). This relationship developed because of his belief in God's promises, promises which were hard to believe.

Yet he did not waver at the promise of God through unbelief, but was strengthened in faith, giving glory to God and being fully convinced that what He had promised He was also able to perform. (Rom. 4:21)

His trust in God was so great that he was able to launch out and believe the unbelievable, see the unseeable, and do the undoable. No wonder he was called a "friend of God."

Faithfulness

Another quality of God's friendship to us is that of steadfastness. The phrase, "His love endures forever," is reiterated numerous times in the book of Psalms, being found in Psalm 100, 106, 107, 118. The concept is also found in many other passages.

157

Earthly friendships are so fragile that imperfections and failures splinter them and cause them to disintegrate. This, however, is untrue of God's friendship. "The Lord is faithful in all his words and gracious in all his deeds" (Psa.145:13)RSV. "A friend loves at all times" (Prov.17:17). This is hypothetical as far as earthly friendships go, but God's friendship is constant. He loves us when we love him, but he also loves us when we are unloving. Andy Ritchie, former Bible professor at Harding University, reminded his students, "If you aren't as close to God as you once were, remember that it's you who has moved, not God."

God's friendship is unmovable. Though our love wanes, his remains. What a contrast with earthly friendships! One violation or infringement and it shatters, not being strong enough to survive. Even the closest ties on earth can be severed by human frailties.

David said in Psalm 27, "When my father and my mother forsake me, then the Lord will take me up." There is no greater friendship than that between parent and child. My mother has been my friend and confidant always. I always hurried home from school to tell her the news of the day, and I wrote daily while in college, as did she. With the wildest stretch of imagination, I could never visualize a circumstance that would cause a rift. Once, however, when I was newly married, young and very thoughtless, I moved out of state and became so busy with a teaching career and new marriage responsibilities I failed to write home or call for an extended period of time. Mother's letters continued to pour in until all at once, obviously offended, she wrote saying, "If you don't want to hear from me anymore, just let me know!" For the first time in my life I realized that

Mother, too, was human. The friendship which I had assumed all my life required something on my part. I had partial responsibility for maintaining this friendship. I wrote an apology for my thoughtlessness and our closeness resumed, but with a new realization that even our friendship, the strongest on earth, could terminate, being based on human weaknesses. "Most men will proclaim each his own goodness, But who can find a faithful man?" (Prov.20:6)

Our friendship with God is stable because one of the two parties remains steadfast. What a blessing we enjoy in having constant access to God's friendship!

God is faithful in being there for us, but is also faithful in "wounding" us if we fail to hold up our end of the friendship. "Faithful are the wounds of a friend" (Prov. 27:6).

Friendship is maintained in most homes by some form of discipline. When growing up I remember Daddy's razor strap hanging on a peg on the wall as a reminder that we would be "wounded" if we did not hold up our end of the friendship. I only remember it coming off its peg once, but its visibility was enough to confirm its purpose and its seriousness.

God has various ways of "wounding" us. David had his Nathan, Saul had his light, Jonah was convicted by a wormy gourd vine. We each receive our wounds in different ways, but whatever the way, those wounds are sufficient to remind us of the urgency of staying in friendship with God.

When we are prodded through discipline back to God he is quick to forgive and to restore our friendship. Represented by the prodigal son's father, God rejoices in our return without censuring, with no "I told you so," or "next time," reminders (Luke 15). It is important to know that we are loved unconditionally. This total acceptance adds the dimension of security to our friendship with God.

Conclusion

Only as we go about our daily lives walking and talking with God , staying in constant friendship with him, will we live life in the fullest sense (1 John 1:7). The constant access to his friendship is one of our greatest blessings, sustaining us in times of loneliness and isolation.

THOUGHTS FOR DISCUSSION

I. Has God disclosed all of his thoughts to man? Read Job 38 and 39 regarding this. Are we capable of understanding all of God's thoughts?

2. Discuss Jesus' choice of close friends and the special relationship they enjoyed.

3. Of what qualities is friendship comprised besides those mentioned in this chapter?

4. Did Jesus show favoritism by selecting 12 best friends?

Prayer Thought: "Oh Lord, how priceless is your friendship!"

Chapter Thirteen

SHOWING HERSELF FRIENDLY

Looking back upon the wealth of human friendships I have enjoyed throughout life I am made to realize what a vital part they have played in my happiness and fruitfulness. Some were so brief they were barely visible, some lasted only a season and were gone, and some are lifelong in nature. Whatever the span of time covered, they were blessings from God, sent for a season and cherished forever. I am sorry to say that my greatest weaknesses lie in my response to these friends, my awareness of their needs, and my ability to touch their lives in meaningful and positive ways as they have touched mine. The study of this subject has brought afresh to my mind the gaping hole left by each friend's absence, and has renewed my determination to imitate my Lord by making the necessary effort to develop and maintain friendships which enhance godliness.

Initiate Friendship
Friendship is a decision. "A man who has friends must himself be friendly"(Prov. 18:24).

Some people seem to have a knack for developing friendships and a magnetism that draws others to them. If we look closely, however, we see that quite an effort was made on their part to initiate and nurture friendship. Friendship building is an art that requires skill. Jesus initiated friendship. He said to his apostles, "You did not choose me, but I chose you" (John 15:16).

Each of us likes to be chosen. It is a compliment to be picked for a friend. I was sitting in an empty dorm room my first night of college with a lump in my throat and a fresh memory of my parents' departure when a girl walked in, introduced herself, and said, "Hi. Let's go to the student center for a coke." I was delighted and that began our long term friendship. We pledged a club together, laughed together, and later wrote letters and shared our traumas and triumphs. Had she not cared enough to instigate the friendship I might never have known her and my life would have been poorer indeed.

Nurture Friendship

Initiating, however, is not enough. Friendship must be nurtured in order to grow. As a friend I must protect and defend, whether it be from circumstances, from others or from self. My daddy had many friends whom he valued greatly and I learned from him what it means to defend his friend in the presence of others. The country store porch was a favorite hangout for neighbors to gather and chat. Several fellows were sitting around on nail kegs chewing tobacco, spitting, and gossiping about a man who had been a long time friend of my daddy. "His fences are torn down, his farm equipment is old, and his barns are falling in. What good to our community is a man like that?" the talk went.

"What's he worth?" "Nothing," chorused the others. "Well," my daddy quickly broke in, "I've never heard him use a bad word, never heard him tell a smutty story, and never heard him criticize or speak a word against his neighbors." The conversation ended. All were quiet.

I learned from that little episode that being a friend implies protecting one's name and being an advocate in presence of attack. When Jesus faced bodily harm Peter rose to his defense with a sword, but when his name came under attack Peter faded into the background denying even knowing him. We are like that at times. When our friends face subtle attack we wince away for fear of our own reputation while we know that a friend defends. "Though one may be overpowered by another two can withstand him" (Eccle. 4:12).

Not only does friendship mean protection from others but also protection from self. We can become our own worst enemies. We set ourselves up for failure. It takes courage to confront and constrain. We each have our own besetting sin and it hurts to say or have another say to us, "In view of your problem do you really think this is a wise course for you to follow?" We risk disfavor when we confront, but Solomon said, "Faithful are the wounds of a friend but the kisses of an enemy are deceitful" (Prov. 27:6). We must care more for the well-being of our friend than for hurt feelings or our own disfavor. People with obsessive, compulsive disorders (spending, shoplifting, gambling or eating) need help in avoiding their point of temptation. Are we being unfriendly when we help steer them away from self-harm?

Be Constant in Friendship

Equally important to friendship is stability, or

164

faithfulness. Being there for our friends is one of the "musts". " Many a man claims to have unfailing love but a faithful man who can find?"(Prov. 25:19)

God is the only one who is the same yesterday, today, and forever, but we aspire to be like God. We don't want our friendship to hinge on moods or approval or disapproval. A friend loves at all times, even when exasperated, or bogged down with work, or disappointed. The availability of our friendship must remain constant. Who wants a friend who is sometimes there and sometimes not? We would then look elsewhere for one to share our confidences and special moments. Solomon likened our reliance on an unfaithful friend to a bad tooth or a lame foot (Prov. 25:19). It is crippling to lean on one whom we expect to be there and find him or her missing. Dependability is essential.

Be Generous

Again, looking to God for example, we learn that he *so loved* that he *gave* (John 3:16). Does friendship imply gift giving? Remember the story of David and Jonathon. Jonathon loved David as his own soul and shed the very clothes from his body to give to David, his friend (1 Sam. 18:1-4).

Special gifts, signifying friendship, are treasures indeed! Among my most valuable possessions are my mother's thimble, given to symbolize our bond of common interest in sewing; my grandmother's vase, a wedding gift received from her dearest friend and passed to me because of our friendship, and a cross stitched poem from a special cousin and friend. I also treasure several unique gifts from my children, including a box of toilet tissue hair bows made by my first two daughters when they were young. Some gifts come in the form of deeds rather than possessions. My son's special interest in my writing and his taking time to teach me computer skills, and patiently reteach again and again was a friendship gesture. So were the meticulously copied recipes (all my favorites which were scribbled on scrap paper) neatly filed in a recipe box given as a surprise from my youngest two daughters. Gifts given out of love and not compulsion are sure signs of friendship.

Blessings of Friendship
Friendship does not come cheap. It costs us time, money and effort, but the many blessings which result make it well worth our effort.

Two are better than one, because they
have a good reward for their labor: For if
they fall, one will lift up his companion. But
woe to him who is alone when he falls, for
he has no one to help him up. (Eccl. 4:10)

Jeremiah had such a friend. He was thrown into a pit of mud and mire where he would have succumbed from starvation and neglect, but a friend, Ebedmelech, perhaps unknown to Jeremiah, went in his behalf to the king. Because of this intervention Jeremiah was lifted from the pit and life was restored (Jer. 38:8-10).

(1)   Encouragement
Not many of us, if any, have sunk into a literal pit of mud and mire as Jeremiah did and experienced the need for a friend such as Ebedmelech to lift us from our death, but many of us have sunk into an emotional or spiritual pit and been retrieved from the depths of self pity, complaint, negativism or despair by a friend.

At a time when my children were busy at their

own thing; one married, two in college, one a high school cheerleader and one engrossed in Jr. High football, I suddenly felt the lack of luster in my own life. I complained to my friend, Jane, about the mundaneness of my work compared to my husband's challenging job with its trips and awards and successes, or to our children's eager expectations for each new day packed with opportunities and excitement. I noted that my time was sure to come; "Every dog has his day," I concluded. "Yes. That's true," she responded, "But has it ever occurred to you that you may have had yours and not recognized it?" This brought us both to laughter. I saw the absurdity of my complaints. God had given me everything: beautiful, laughing children full of love for me and each other, a dependable, godly mate whom I adored, friends to surround me, and I was complaining about mundaneness! My friend had lifted me up from the sin of negativism.

(2) Productivity

The levity of a friend adds spice to life. Fresh ideas, spiritual insights, discussions on home management, projects such as garage sales, home perms, and shopping excursions can result from brainstorming sessions. "As iron sharpens iron, so one man sharpens another"(Prov. 27:17). A friend can stimulate the wit, the intellect, and the productivity . As Solomon said, "they have a good return for their work"(Eccle. 4:10).

Shakespeare noted the positive effect one friend can have on another. "But if the while I think on thee, dear friend, all losses are restored and sorrows end."[1] Spirits are lifted and burdens lightened in the presence of a friend.

(3) Warmth

" Again if two lie down together, they will keep warm. But how can one be warm alone?"(Eccle. 4:11). There is nothing colder that loneliness. The memory of the friendship of my sisters triggers feelings of warmth as I remember the coziness of our bed on cold, winter nights with our legs wrapped snugly around each other enjoying the warmth and security. When they married and I was left to sleep alone I remember the loneliness that was connected with the cold bed and I was aware of all those who had not enjoyed the friendship of a sister, a friendship which has added warmth to many areas of life.

Even pets offer a hint of friendship because of the warmth they afford. It has been found that people live longer if they have pets to help fill the gap incurred by loneliness in old age. How much healthier and happier is it then to have human friends?

Caution in Friendship

Just any friend will not do. God gives warnings about nonproductive friendships, noting that anyone who chooses to be a friend of the world becomes his enemy (James 4:4). "The righteous should choose his friends carefully" (Prov. 12:26). A friend by nature is one who will wield a profound influence on us by example as well as by persuasion. If that friend is not looking to God for direction in life I could be enticed away from godliness through his influence. "Evil company corrupts good habits" (I Cor. 15:33).

Others mentioned in the category with the world are fools, gluttons, and prostitutes. (Prov. 13:20, 28:7, and 29:3.) They may influence us subtly by making the world look appealing. We are never too young or old to need the good influence of friends, or to be affected by the bad.

We have a special warning about making friends with hot tempered men. "Make no friendship with an angry man, and with a furious man do not go, Lest you learn his ways and set a snare for your soul" (Prov. 22:24,25) . While a soft answer turns away wrath, harsh words stir up anger. If we do not want our anger stirred we need to avoid the source of contention.

Opportunities for Friendship

Knowing whom to befriend is important. Access to friendship is all around us. Sometimes we overlook the wealth of friendship potential in our family circles. I once read a story about a woman who was troubled because of her deficit in friendships. She had read that every woman should have at least three strong friendships in order to be fulfilled. She was constantly involved at home with her husband and children. There was no time for luncheons since her husband came in daily for lunch. Shopping sprees were out because the money allocated for shopping was limited to Saturday trips to the mall with her daughters in search of necessary clothes and school supplies. Upon further examination of her full schedule, however, she realized that she had three close friends: a husband and two daughters with whom she loved spending time.

If we have established friendship relationships in the home then we are among the blessed! These friendships are constant and accessible. They go with us wherever we go and are lifelong in nature.

Friendship between sisters can be the strongest in the world. They may have conflicts that appear to be of great magnitude, but their love for each other is even greater. Our daughters (affectionately named Number One and Number Three by their daddy) had their share of conflicts. These were revealed through betraying confidences, embarrassing each other in public, and occasionally competing for the same boyfriend. I was concerned that these conflicts were so grave their love for each other would be marred forever. However, when they were grown they clung to each other, spent hours on the phone, visited back and forth even though they were separated by 600 miles, and became confidantes. Theresa (Number One) had one adopted child and a record of miscarriages while Matilda (Number Three) had five children including twins. Matilda found it too hard to be given her heart's desire and to have her sister denied so, with her husband's consent, she volunteered to go to the invitro clinic in Atlanta and try to carry a baby for Theresa. The sight of that minivan loaded with Mother, Daddy, and five small children heading for Atlanta with prospects of going through a traumatic experience was a sight I will not forget. Even though the efforts failed to result in a baby, that offer of love will be cherished forever. There is a special bond between those two families that obliterated all childhood conflict. What friendship could be stronger than that of sisters?

In-law relationships, contrary to popular belief, can afford great friendship. Ruth and Naomi portrayed the ideal picture of friends (Ruth 1:6-8). Their love for each other stretched beyond the normal call of duty and sustained them in life's lowest ebbs. I am familiar with this type of strong in-law friendship. My husband, Dean, and my daddy enjoyed such a one. From the first time Daddy met Dean, my husband-to-be, he loved him with a passion. Daddy had reared three girls and lost two sons so he had missed having someone with whom to share his interests which lay in the masculine realm. He loved Dean's beautiful baritone voice but he loved even more his ability to drive a tractor, break and work a garden, and cut wood. They enjoyed thirty two years of working together, traveling together and even shopping together. Dean took him to Houston to see the Astrodome when he was 73. When he was 90 they went to Atlanta to see the Civil War sights and the battlegrounds where my daddy's father had fought. They did their Christmas shopping together a day or so before Christmas each year and really got into the spirit of the season buying last minute gifts, choosing a turkey and occasionally returning home in a snow storm enjoying the pioneer spirit. Daddy helped instill in Dean the love of the scriptures and of the heroes in the Bible as he sat for hours talking his favorite subject. Dean helped him with the garden and with house upkeep and in his last days he played nursemaid to him in the hospital when cancer had so overtaken him that he couldn't swallow. Dean sat by his bed and swabbed his mouth with soothing ointment, massaging his gums and raw sores to give him relief. I heard Daddy say in a whisper, "Dean, you've done more for me than any doctor." I thanked God in my heart for their rare friendship which had been full of blessings for each.

Conclusion

Friendship is not bound by age or gender. It cuts across all lines and makes itself available in surprising ways, but our greatest opportunity for friendship is with God. Hopefully, as youth we are being taught in the home and in the church about God, our friend. We learn to pray to him and recognize him to be a great resource in our lives even though we rely heavily on our parents for most of our necessary provisions and care. As we grow older we learn to transfer our dependency on parents to a dependency on God so that by the teenage years God, our friend, has become very important. During these crucial years we face many temptations, and we need his friendship to sustain us and protect us from the strong influences of our peers. There are things we can tell him that we cannot tell anybody else and we know he will honor our confidentiality. There are many occasions when our parents are not there to shield and defend us, but if we rely on God during these times he becomes our closest friend.

With the responsibilities of adulthood comes again the urgency of a strong friendship with God. There are so many things we do not know and wisdom is always available from him. Strength is limited and the childrearing business demanding, but God sustains us during those sleepless nights and empowers us during the day with the necessary energy to accomplish our work and train our little ones. His friendship is so vital during these times.

As our parents, who have been power sources in our lives, grow older and die, we began to feel our resources diminishing and God's friendship becomes even more essential every day. We realize that other resources will continue to diminish until one day God may be the only one left to sustain us. His friendship has become more and more meaningful after having walked with him through so many stages of life and having always felt his presence very near. As our friendship with him mellows and ripens some day, hopefully, each of us will be able to say like David, "Though I walk through the valley of the shadow of death,

I will fear no evil for You are with me" (Psa. 23:4).

1. Shakespeare, "Sonnet 30," *Riverside Shakespeare* (Boston, Mass.: Houghton Mifflin, 1974), pp. 1754-1755.

THOUGHTS FOR DISCUSSION

1. Do we show partiality when we select certain people to be our closest friends or should all fellow Christians get the same treatment?
2. What extra responsibilities do we assume, if any, when we claim friendship with a person?
3. Can circumstances arise which would necessitate the severance of a friendship? If so, discuss the circumstances.
4. Discuss Proverbs 27:6 regarding the wounds of a friend. How can these wounds be used for spiritual growth?

Prayer Thought: "Enrich our lives with friends, dear God, and help us to be a constant source of strength and encouragement to them."